A Pedagogy for Planetary *Convivência*

"This is a book written from the heart of a Brazilian woman, a Christian critical educator. Its message communicates across cultures and traditions a compelling and radically inclusive vision of life together—*convivência*—with reconciliation with each other and healing and wholeness for the earth as well. With a prophetic vocation, Débora Junker invites us to join her in a movement to enact an alternative pedagogy of care and justice; that is, an education that nurtures emotional, socio-political and spiritual intelligence, and moral discernment aimed at wholesome living (*buen vivir*). The reason for the resonance of her message is that it addresses our deepest longing for truth and meaning, communion and connectedness, and for life giving and community building life projects. This book is a gift of fresh, distinct and indispensable material in the ever-growing Freirean corpus. And Débora Junker offers it with courage, wisdom, and grace. I strongly recommend it!"

—**Daniel S. Schipani**, professor emeritus of pastoral care and counseling, Anabaptist Mennonite Biblical Seminary

"*A Pedagogy for Planetary Convivência* by Junker emerges as a profound call to the heart and spirit of our collective consciousness, deeply rooted in feminist theology of care from the Global South and Freirean critical pedagogy. The book, crafted with tenderness and fierce passion, invites us into a sacred dialogue between the soul of the Earth and the essence of human interconnectedness. Junker weaves a vibrant tapestry of personal stories and scholarly wisdom, advocating for an educational praxis that embraces compassion, justice, and ecological integrity as pillars of global citizenship. The book is Junker's clarion call to embrace our inherent interconnectedness with both the planet and one another, urging us to cultivate a pedagogy that is both liberatory and deeply grounded in the nurturing of life in all its forms. A must-read for those who stand at the intersection of faith, human wholeness, and the fight for a just and sustainable world, Junker's work guides us toward a transformative *convivência* that honors the divine in every creature and the sacredness of our shared home."

—**Boyung Lee**, professor of practical theology, Illif School of Theology

"Offering the powerful image of reconnecting us to the 'flow of the rivers of life,' Débora Junker invites us into a holistic conversation about 'care-full' transformative education. I recommend we journey with her. Not only does she provide a dialogue with a cross-continental group of social philosophers, critical educators, and theologians, but also she passionately and poetically demonstrates how feelings, care, solidarity, lovingness, and community are at the heart of critical reflection and social change."

—**Jack Seymour**, professor emeritus of religious education, Garrett-Evangelical Theological Seminary

"Grounded in a contemplative Christian spirituality, an insightful grasp of Freirean thought, and an evident interfaith, interreligious, and ecumenical tone, coupled with diverse cultural contexts, this book is a timely response to a world that is in desperate need for civil sensibilities that are laced with compassion, care, and dialogical spaces. Débora Junker provides a pathway toward navigating those sensibilities in a stylistically approachable manner that stirs one to reflect, inspiring to tangibly participate in fostering a more loving, just, and kind planet."

—**James D. Kirylo**, professor of curriculum theory, critical pedagogy, and literacy, University of South Carolina

A Pedagogy for Planetary *Convivência*

A Freirean Perspective to Think Pedagogy Otherwise

Débora B. A. Junker

Foreword by Donaldo Macedo

◆PICKWICK *Publications* · Eugene, Oregon

A PEDAGOGY FOR PLANETARY CONVIVÊNCIA
A Freirean Perspective to Think Pedagogy Otherwise

Copyright © 2025 Débora B. A. Junker. All rights reserved. Except for brief quotations in critical publications or reviews, no part of this book may be reproduced in any manner without prior written permission from the publisher. Write: Permissions, Wipf and Stock Publishers, 199 W. 8th Ave., Suite 3, Eugene, OR 97401.

Pickwick Publications
An Imprint of Wipf and Stock Publishers
199 W. 8th Ave., Suite 3
Eugene, OR 97401

www.wipfandstock.com

PAPERBACK ISBN: 978-1-62564-222-6
HARDCOVER ISBN: 978-1-4982-8672-5
EBOOK ISBN: 978-1-7252-4883-0

Cataloguing-in-Publication data:

Names: Junker, Débora B. A., author. | Macedo, Donaldo P. (Donaldo Pereira), 1950–, foreword.

Title: A pedagogy for planetary convivência : a Freirean perspective to think pedagogy otherwise / Débora B. A. Junker.

Description: Eugene, OR: Pickwick Publications, 2025. | Includes bibliographical references and index.

Identifiers: ISBN 978-1-62564-222-6 (paperback). | ISBN 978-1-4982-8672-5 (hardcover). | ISBN 978-1-7252-4883-0 (ebook).

Subjects: LSCH: Critical Pedagogy. | Freire, Paulo, 1921–1997—Criticism, interpretation, etc. | Conviviality.

Classification: LB880 F73 J85 2025 (print). | LB880 (epub).

VERSION NUMBER 01/29/25

Cover Art: *Salvaguardar—Somos mundos num só* (Safeguard—We are worlds in one), black ink, 2024
By Yohana Agra Junker
Cover design: Rafael Ferreira

Scripture quotations are taken from the New Revised Standard Version Bible © 1989 by the Division of Christian Education of the National Council of the Churches of Christ in the United States of America. Used by permission. All rights reserved.

*To our grandchildren, Alice & Hugo.
In the hope that the waters of affection can bathe your existence and
all children will have the right to peaceful coexistence.*

Contents

Foreword by Donaldo Macedo | ix
Acknowledgments | xix

Introduction | 1
1 The Heart of Education and the Education of the Heart | 15
2 *Buen Vivir* towards a Planetary *Convivência* | 27
3 Social Responsibility for Planetary *Convivência* | 50
4 Care-full Education: Resisting a Culture of Care-lessness | 69
5 Principles to *Sulear* Our Pedagogies | 94
6 A Pedagogy Otherwise: Cartography of Affections | 127

Bibliography | 145
Index | 153

Foreword

A PEDAGOGY FOR PLANETARY *Convivência* (conviviality) is a ray of hope in a world of unmatched cruelty against a targeted group of people whose only sin is to be Palestinian and thus deemed not worthy of humanity. While Débora Junker's book does not focus on the ongoing genocide of Palestinians in Gaza, it equips readers with a wealth of critical tools with which they can deconstruct the colonial ideology so as to more clearly demonstrate that the scourge of colonialism did not die with the independence of former colonies in most of the world: it is disastrously employed in Gaza where racism is the organizing principle to relegate Palestinians as sub humans or "animals" as the current Israel Minister of Defense, Yoav Gallant, put it. Once categorized as "human animals," the act of ethnic cleansing in the name of religion is justified where God's chosen people can slaughter more than 28,000 Palestinians of which 15,000 are children, all the while claiming that it is for the humanity's own good.

Junker's book is also a ray of hope in that she provides more than a language of critique which can be used to deconstruct the ideology that attempts to normalize the slaughter of children as the necessary price to make sure that the blood of the chosen people remain "pure" and untainted. The significance of *A Pedagogy for Planetary Convivência* lies not only in the denunciation of all forms of inhumanity, but in Junker's uncompromising embrace of what it really means to be fully human, as she pushes readers to gain a greater understanding of how a language of possibility can be one which is steeped in love. This book thus offers alternative ways of being in the world and with the world. In other words, along the lines of Freirean ideals, Junker's language of critique is neither devoid of interconnectedness

Foreword

nor pure "verbalism that lacks action."[1] Rather, it is a language of critique that must always be followed by "reflection on action"[2] and whose motivating principle is love and its ability to make the world more harmonious and less dehumanizing.

Readers of this book will understand that it is not enough to engage in an uncompromising rejection of the colonial DNA that generates, guides, and shapes the professed "civilization" of Western powers currently being promoted and justified by the United States of America—a nation whose platitudes of liberty, democracy, and equality ring hollow for its victims. Though its victims voice their struggle, Malcolm X once lamented the "white man . . . is going to talk the pretty talk, but he will still continue to practice those inhuman deeds."[3] Despite the concerted efforts of the civil rights movement, Malcolm X predicted the white man will continue to deny African-Americans the right to vote if he can, he will continue to curtail their freedom, and he will continue to deny African-Americans equality, all of which translates into the denial of their full humanity. The vacuousness of the American "pretty words" of democratic values was not lost on the over 10,000 Iraqis, mostly civilians, who perished in the American bombardment of Mosul in Iraq when the U.S. and its allies waged their attack as an alleged defense against terrorism, normalizing the terror exacted by the state on civilians as non-terror but as a needed "civilizing" act. The critical ability to connect historical events, often obfuscated by "pretty words," can equip people with a conscience. Those who care about history's lessons can easily comprehend that behind the "self-righteousness" of the right for self-defense lies a more macabre and surreal reality of genocide, as we have witnessed taking place in real time in Gaza. The question that the Western powers refuse to raise is: do the Palestinians who have been occupied and under siege have the right to self-defense against Israel's occupation of their land for over 75 years or do Palestinians have the right to aspire their liberation and freedom?

The brilliance of *A Pedagogy for Planetary Convivência* also lies in offering a counterpoint to despair despite its unwavering confrontation with truth. The author's keen insight begins with a refusal to accept the often-promoted Western fragmentation of knowledge that invariably gives rise

1. Freire, *Politics of Education*, 11.
2. Freire, *Politics of Education*, 11.
3. Medrut, "Inspirational Quotes from Malcolm X" (https://www.goalcast.com/malcolm-x-quotes/).

Foreword

to false binarism where scientific pursuits, in the name of total objectivity, must squeeze out the fundamental essence of human knowledge: emotions. This fragmented form of knowledge masquerades as the only truth, often wrapped in "pretty words" though denying the role of emotions in the comprehension of other knowledges; it gives rise to the usual cultural reproduction which, in turn, normalizes hyper individualism, isolation, and the illusion of the self as the center of the universe. Putting aside the psychological ramifications of fostering pathologies such as narcissism, the fragmentation of knowledge or reality blocks any possibility of *convivência* (conviviality) in which harmony and solidarity—action rooted in a sense of empathy and justice—can emerge. Humans, in their very act of conviviality, must acknowledge their interconnectedness, not only with each other, but also with the planet whose bounty and beauty sustain life. Thus, instead of exacerbating the pollution and the ongoing rape of the land, a justly organized society must be premised on humility. Market-driven societies must de-prioritize their insatiable need to meet the next quarter's revenues through which both things and human endeavors are always commodified and neatly prepackaged for a profitable sale. In the callous neoliberal calculus, market forces view humans as mere merchandise, a posture firmly rejected by Junker as she presents an alternative grounded in human relationship:

> For *convivência* to emerge, however, mutual flourishing is fundamental—there must be no place for invisibility, indifference, and disregard. On the contrary, the idea of *convivência* that I'm attempting to communicate suggests an orientation toward and bond formed between individuals who regularly and closely interact with one another. This *convivência* proposes that individuals or communities must develop the ability to understand differences without feeling the need to fix them. The art of living together must allow inconsistencies, ambiguity, and discrepancies to exist alongside one another without being divisive or exclusionary. It cherishes human connections and focuses on the principles of collaboration and building reciprocal trust. As a fundamentally relational concept, *convivência* emphasizes the importance of being with others, and becoming with one another instead of striving to live a life based on individualism.[4]

In essence, *A Pedagogogy for Planetary Conviviência* embraces Paulo Freire's spirit of a radical democracy, which is steeped in dialogue where people

---

4. See p. 30, below.

speak *with* rather than *to* others in a space where the ability to listen is just as central as speaking. Thus, dialogue is *sine qua non* in societies that prioritize *convivência*, as it enables people "to enter into a place where all can be and become who they truly are, despite the dissonances that may unfold [and] can serve as a radical alternative to the ocean of disengagement, indifference, and competition that is drowning our relations to ourselves, each other, and the planet"; *convivência* offers a language for collective feeling and thinking through the "inherent paradox of conflict and harmony, rigidity and fluidity, despair and hope."[5] It is the unconquerable presence of hope that enables people, even when they find themselves in dire circumstances, to move beyond an imposed object position so they can take history into their own hands and become the subjects of history, making, re-making, and transforming it into love rather than hate. Hence, love must always be the operating principle in all human endeavor as it serves as a constant reminder that hate sucks humans of the fundamental essence of their humanity, which is love—a notion that became central to Freire's life and work during his last ten years on this earth.

It is the current unmoored hatred that is putting the world at the precipice of violent apocalypse as leaders of powerful nations reject dialogue, opting instead for the continuation of the colonial project that, at least for the Western nations, began with the age of "discovery"—a misnomer to the degree that the indigenous people who occupied the lands that were claimed as "discovered" never thought of themselves as being lost. No wonder Senator DeSantis of Florida is so busily promoting laws that prevent all students, but particularly students who continue to experience subordination due to their nonwhite status, from learning that their ancestors were dehumanized by the conquerors in order to legitimize the commercialization of humans as slaves and the wholesale killing of natives. If students do not have historical knowledge, then they will not know about the horrific acts throughout U.S. history which constituted crimes against humanity—crimes that continue to this day, aided and abetted by a revisionist history championed by the Bible-carrying Christians who support mass killings of children in Gaza but engage in prayers and in violence against abortion clinics as they posture for their pro-life brand. They hope that the prayers make it easier to practice a pedagogy of willful denial of the blood bath that really occurred during the "discovery age" while the despotic monarchs of the conquering countries kept busy building bigger and greater cathedrals

---

5. See p. 31, below.

Foreword

with the gold and riches acquired in the "killing fields" of the newly "discovered" land—pompous cathedrals where they pompously prayed to assuage their guilt for the carnage that yielded the gold that enriched them.

There is a monster lurking in the room when history fails to acknowledge how the "glorious" discovery age was driven by the sole goal of enriching the Western conquering countries. People do not know that the monster working to glorify this destructive past is colonial ideology—a whitewashing process made more insidious for its ability to remain invisible so both the oppressor and the oppressed alike are taught domination is right. Inculcated with the do-gooder narrative that oppression is "for your own good," humanism is emptied of meaning and substituted with "humanitarianism" which, according to Freire, smacks of a false generosity. For Freire, this is a form of charity that "begins with the egoistic interests of the oppressors (an egoism cloaked in the false generosity of paternalism) and makes the oppressed the objects of its humanitarianism, [but] itself maintains and embodies oppression. It is an instrument of dehumanization."[6] Humanitarian charity is less about help for the oppressed than about covering the blood-soaked oppressors in a cloak of innocence. This false generosity not only tolerates cruelty, but exonerates cruelty exacted against people as being "for their own good." Such a notion of the oppressor's "gift" was exemplified in the trial brought by E. Jean Carroll, a former Elle Magazine columnist, against former President Trump, who was found guilty of rape and ordered to pay Carroll $83 million. Trump's defense lawyer, Alina Habba, implied that the rape experienced was for Ms. Carroll's own good since, according to Habba, E. Jean Carroll "has gained more fame, more notoriety than she could have ever dreamed of."

On a nation-state level, the genocide of Palestinians in real time by Israel is defended by its supporters who imply that getting rid of Hamas is ultimately good for Palestinians, given that Hamas and any Palestinians who support its regime are "animals"; a genocide that gets rid of Palestinian "animals" must be "good for" those who survive the indiscriminate carpet bombing of Gaza which, at the time of this writing, has killed over 28,000 Palestinians, mostly civilians, including 15,000 children. Had it not been for the invisibility of the monster in guiding Israel's policy of achieving the Zionist goal of a "Greater Israel," which is predicated on the total replacement of the centuries-long inhabitants of Gaza, or, as some leaders boast, to make Gaza uninhabitable, then how can one explain the wonton slaughter

---

6. Freire, *Pedagogy of Indignation*, xxii.

Foreword

of Palestinians? How it is possible to believe Israel's actions represent anything other than collective punishment and the ethnic cleansing of all Palestinians? It has become evident that behind these actions lies the same dehumanizing ideology that undergirds American aspirations for empire, as President Biden greenlights the obscene slaughter of Palestinians by Israel in the name of so-called self-defense that justifies, in a span of three months, the killing of over 15,000 children. Not only have most leaders of "civilized" Western countries remain silent regarding the genocide taking place in real time, but some of these countries have also exacted cruel punishments against citizens who have joined a growing chorus worldwide calling for a cease fire: those critical of the war have lost their jobs, had their art exhibitions cancelled, and had awards they previously received retracted. While President Biden assures Israeli leaders that "there is no redline" as to the degree of their colonial savageness, he assuages his conscience by going, religiously, to church every Sunday. Both American and Israeli supporters of the Zionists' project remain unable "to break free from the colonial mindset of believing they are possessors of knowledge, a gift from God, and constantly teaching others without learning from them."[7] This mindset, as Junker elucidates, is based on a "paternalistic objective [that] has, by and large, failed in view of the spiritual values and morals that religion is charged to teach,"[8] namely that it is a fallacy to claim knowledge that God would order the total replacement of all Palestinians from their land so as to make room for the creation of "a greater Israel" by any means necessary. Once again the colonial monster rears its head to justify taking the land where Palestinians have lived for centuries to be rebuilt by Jewish settlers from all over the world who are authorized by the state of Israel to steal houses, businesses, and farmlands from Palestinians who are, after all, according to Israel's deputy defense minister, Ben Dahan, who is also a rabbi, "human animals"—that is, nonhumans. As such, the implication for those Palestinians who survive the genocide is that they would be corralled in barbwire-fenced concentration camps, certainly in an almost demolished Gaza, and patrolled by God's chosen soldiers who unabashedly celebrate by dancing and singing after a Palestinian village and its inhabitants are reduced to ashes.

The important insights of Junker's book, *A Pedagogy for Planetary Convivência*, demonstrate her keen ability to provide readers with

---

7. See p. 3, below.
8. See p. 3, below.

Foreword

a language of critique which, in turn, can denude the "civilizing acts" of highly developed nations that are used as mere cover for their "insatiable quest for power and control through which new forms of colonialism are engendered through institutions."[9] How else can one explain how highly educated individuals can be so indoctrinated that they cannot see the level of carnage carried out in the name of religion, as in the case of Israel, and in the name of democracy when the United States provides Israel with fighter jets and tons and tons of guided and unguided bombs to rain over the heads of Palestinian civilians? What is justified as Israel's right to self-defense is, in reality, cruel bombing with abandon that seeks the complete destruction of Gaza and anyone and anything the breathes in this very narrow strip of Palestine. The unnerving silence among the Western leaders regarding Israel's slaughter of Palestinians is in obscene contrast with the unrelenting castigation of Russia by the same Western leaders who, in the name of democracy, offer unlimited military and other material support to Ukraine, including quasi open borders that welcome Ukraine refugees while calling Putin a war criminal, a murderer. How many of these same countries are making similar offers to Palestinians in despair with no place to hide and who are facing a slow death by starvation if they are lucky enough to evade the destructive carpet bombing to which they are being subjected?

Let me make it very clear that my critique of the right-wing Israeli government and the U.S. right-leaning leadership that have made the genocide of Palestinians possible should not be cudgeled using the generalized tropes of antisemitism and un-Americanism. These overused tropes are, in my view, astute tactics marshalled by the propaganda apparatus of these two nations. As Noam Chomsky, who is Jewish, so often points out, only totalitarian states use these censorship mechanisms to block any form of critique. In an allegedly free society such as the United States, characterizing a critique of President Biden's policies of war in Gaza as un-American borders on ridiculousness. What it also does is to point to the totalitarian colonial propensity of the current U.S. administration. As for labelling a critique of Israeli leaders and their policies as "antisemitism," this serves to make dissent more difficult, especially given the ugly history of antisemitism all over the world, particularly among the Western nations. When any critique of Israeli leaders is immediately countered by the antisemitism label, even when the critique is presented by Jewish people themselves, the automatic label is never to describe the views being expressed as anti-Israel

9. See p. 4, below.

Foreword

but the people speaking as "Jew haters." While critique of Israeli leadership may earn the incorrect antisemitic label, to remain silent in view of the current war crimes against humanity being committed in Gaza is to ensure one's complicity with these horrendous crimes. Consequently, the critiques must always be contextualized and done cogently so as to leave no breathing room for countercharges that are designed to brook no dissent and have already cost the Presidents of Harvard and University of Pennsylvania their jobs—just for not displaying strong enough public support for Israel.

Junker's inspiring book, *A Pedagogy for Planetary Convivência*, will certainly join the long list of banned books American students are not allowed to read in order to keep them from gaining the critical tools that would debunk the myth of American exceptionalism. Although one might define this exceptionalism as an imperialist desire that exceedingly surpasses the nation's former colonial penchant for cruelty, inhumanity, and grotesque greed, we are helpfully reminded by Howard Zinn that this is the real history of America: "In the course of westward expansion, the new nation, the United States, stole the Indians' land, killed them when they resisted, destroyed their source of food and shelter, pushed them into smaller and smaller sections of the country, and went about the systematic destruction of Indian society.... [The stealing in the 1830s] of millions of acres from the Indians ... [was referred by] Lewis Cass, the governor of Michigan territory ... as the progress of civilization ... [since a] barbarous people cannot live in contact with a civilized community."[10]

Fast-forward to the 2020s, and *A Pedagogy for Planetary Convivência* provides readers with myriad critical tools that enable readers to understand why it is fundamental to contextualize historical events in order to comprehend why the more things change, the more they stay the same. Hence, when historical events are contrasted and juxtaposed, we begin to develop a clear picture why Israeli leaders aggressively want to erase the 75-year history of Palestinian life under occupation. Through a sophisticated propaganda apparatus, they prefer that the media focus the world's attention on the horrendous attack by Hamas "that killed more than 1,200 Israelis and foreign nationals, mostly civilians [and that] more than 240 hostages were snatched and spirited to Gaza, where they have reportedly languished in abysmal conditions."[11] This horrific act of violence makes October 7, 2023 a day of infamy for all Israelis and the world, a collective loss of life through

---

10. Zinn and Macedo, *Howard Zinn on Democratic Education*, 114.
11. Schlein, "WHO: Gaza Cut Off from Food, Water."

Foreword

violence that constitutes a crime against humanity. Denouncing this tragic loss of innocent lives is imperative for all who consider themselves part of a civilized world. Yet, as Noam Chomsky pointed out in our dialogue in 2000, "western intellectuals . . . have no problems applying elementary moral principles in cases that involve official enemies."[12] What is more difficult but no less imperative is applying the same "elementary moral principles" to hold Israel to account for its defense minister, Yoav Gallant, who ordered "a full siege" of the Gaza Strip, adding that "no power, no food, no gas" will reach Palestinian territory.[13] This policy will entail a guaranteed slow death sentence for Palestinians through starvation and disease, even while they are being showered by tons upon tons of bombs from jet fighters that have made northern Gaza uninhabitable by destroying hospitals, schools, and 70% of houses, many of them occupied by the entire families. Gallant is, in essence, putting into practice the settler colonial strategy described by Lewis Cass, the governor of Michigan in the 1830s, when he concluded that the stealing of Indian land by American settlers and the savagery of killing that followed each act of Indian resistance to what was perceived by these settlers as "civilizing acts" reflected an inevitable progression, since the settlers could not co-exist with the barbarous Indians who did not acquiesce to the robbing of their land and the slaughter of their people. The Israel Defense Minister's rationale for the implementation of genocide in Gaza adheres to the time-worn colonial project that must always dehumanize the victims of occupation as "human animals" with whom co-existence is abhorrent.

Dehumanization of human beings who are different along race and ethnicity is racism, a central principle of colonialism. Gaza is an example par excellence that colonialism has never been eradicated, even as Nazism was not eliminated with the defeat of Germany and has seen a resurgence in many forms in too many countries. What should be clear to people is that bombs will not put an end to the ideology of hate. *A Pedagogy for Planetary Convivência* provides a clear road map that love, and hope is where hate goes to die. This shift of heart is eloquently captured by the prominent Palestinian poet, Refaat Alareer, who was murdered by an Israel airstrike in Gaza, joining now over 28,000 other Palestinians who have died at the hands of Israel's machinery of death.[14] While Refaat was murdered, the

---

12. Chomsky, *Chomsky on Miseducation*, 12.
13. Gallant quoted in Ray, "No Electricity, No Food, No Fuel."
14. *Democracy Now!*, "Palestinian Poet Mosab Abu Toha."

Foreword

military might of Israel was not able to kill the hope that fueled his soul and the love he emanated in life and in his poetry. His orphaned children will never forget him since his love is etched in their memory as it is also etched in the hearts of all those who consider themselves fully human. While his body decomposes under the rubble, his poetry birthed love and hope into the world as he, humanly, had wished but was denied:

> If I must die
> let it bring hope
> let it be a tale.[15]

—Donaldo Macedo

---

15. *Democracy Now!*, "If I Must Die."

Acknowledgments

IN THE GRAND NARRATIVE of bringing a book to life, countless characters play integral roles behind the scenes. To each of you, I owe an immeasurable debt of gratitude that mere words can scarcely capture. Yet, I attempt to express my appreciation with heartfelt sincerity.

First and foremost, I extend my deepest thanks to my unwavering source of love, strength, and inspiration: my family. To my beloved husband, Tércio, your steadfast support and encouragement have kept my balance through the ups and downs of this process. Your belief in me has been a light through the long days and nights of writing and your calm presence in moments of doubt. To our children, Yohana, Louise, and Tércio A., your resilience, kindheartedness, and accomplishments are sources of inspiration and appreciation. Your love reminds me of what truly matters in life, and for that, I am forever grateful.

To my parents—Zayde, my prayer warrior, and Luciano (*in memoriam*)—your boundless love and unwavering belief in my potential have been the cornerstone of my journey. Your sacrifices and endless encouragement have fueled my fortitude to pursue my dreams. And to my beloved family, including my ancestors, parents, siblings, aunts, cousins, nieces, and all the members of my extended family. Your generosity, laughter, endurance, and compassion have sustained me through many circumstances in life.

I am grateful to my esteemed colleagues, students, and staff at Garrett-Evangelical Theological Seminary. Each interaction with you has left an indelible mark on my intellectual journey and life. Your support as conversation partners has offered valuable insights and inspiration and provided support at various points during this process.

Acknowledgments

I am profoundly grateful to Donaldo Macedo, one of Freire's friends and collaborators, for writing a compassionate foreword. Donaldo's willingness to accept the task and his ability to read between the lines and the languages I used to convey my thoughts and feelings left me humbled and immensely thankful.

I am thankful to Henry Carrigan, who saw the initial spark of an idea and embarked on the painstaking editing process that helped the manuscript take form. I also extend my heartfelt thanks to my publisher, George Callihan, and the dedicated team behind the scenes. Your patience, flexibility, and unwavering commitment to excellence have brought this book to fruition.

I will be remiss if I fail to name and thank four exceptional scholars who generously sacrificed their time and energy to read my book in manuscript form. I thank them for their gracious and valuable feedback. These scholars include Daniel Schipani, Boyung Lee, Jack Seymour, and James Kirylo.

To Yohana, I want to express my sincere gratitude for her sensitivity and artistic talent in capturing the book's essence through images. Your work truly speaks to my heart. I appreciate your trust in your intuitive gift, despite only having an overview of the chapters. Your art is a means of grace, potency, and joy. I would also like to thank Rafael for working with you and doing the design work diligently and precisely. Thank you both for your outstanding contributions to the project.

I want to express my sincere gratitude to all those who have contributed to my journey, visibly and invisibly. Whether you offered a word of encouragement, a listening ear, or invaluable assistance, your contributions have not gone unnoticed. I would also like to extend my heartfelt appreciation to my mentors, Nelle Slater, Linda Vogel, and Rufus Burrow, who are no longer with us. Their lives continue to inspire me to this day. This book is a testament to the power of our collective efforts and bears the imprint of every one of you.

To my readers, I extend my deepest gratitude to all who have joined me on this journey. I hope this book's contents will not just strike a chord with you but also motivate you and contribute in some small way to changing how we live on this planet. Your role in this journey is crucial, and I hope the stories contained within these pages will stay with you long after you turn the final page.

Acknowledgments

Because humans and more-than-humans are interconnected and part of a big family, I express my gratitude to the Earth, our first womb, for its continuous generosity and exuberance manifested through its rivers, forests, skies, and oceans, which offer us shelter and embrace.

Above all, I express my deepest gratitude to God—the Creator of everything—who breathes into us the breath of life and invites us to co-inspire together.

With heartfelt thanks

Débora

Introduction

> "Go into yourself. Find out the reason that commands you to write; see whether it has spread its roots into the very depths of your heart; confess to yourself whether you would have to die if you were forbidden to write. This most of all: ask yourself in the most silent hour of your night: must I write?"
>
> —Rainer Maria Rilke

DECIDING ON A TOPIC to write a book on is not easy for most of us. Of course, some talented people can quickly transform a protocol or proceedings material into a manuscript. Yet, writing is a much more complex process for most of us. It takes time, inspiration, and perseverance. The journey that has brought me here has been neither straightforward nor easy. It was sometimes circuitous or interrupted; at other times, it was dismissed, avoided, or suppressed. When I follow the advice of the poet, whose eyes see beyond the veil of the ordinary, I take the courage to search the depths of my heart and find the reasons in my soul that compel me to write this book.

As the reader will see in the following pages, the subject matter treated in them took root in my being. That is, my commitment to write this book was birthed in the heart—a heart replete with empathy for the less fortunate in the world, outraged by wars in which the killing of children are normalized. Although the way I convey the message that springs from my heart may be imperfect and incomplete, it is out of my most profound concern and love for this world and all humans and more-than-humans who inhabit it. From this sense of commitment and love, I invite you to join me on this journey to dream of a better and more harmonious world.

Earlier in the process of writing, I had the great joy of spending a short time in a Franciscan Retreat Center. During my time there, I was welcomed by wonderful Franciscan sisters who took an interest in my life and the reasons that brought me into their "home." At every meal a sister, or a group of them, would join me to break bread together or would invite me to join their table. During those times, I had the opportunity to rehearse articulating why I was there and share about my writing project. During many conversations with them, the book's content became more defined and more appealing to me. At that time, I was interested in reflecting on how religious education could and should contribute to a broader understanding of citizenship and social responsibility and how educational institutions, both religious and non-religious, could educate their students in that direction. Although a reasonable amount of time has passed between my encounter with the sisters and the conclusion of this project, I have had the chance to reflect more deeply on the principles required to educate for a better coexistence. I am pleased to see how the topic has taken root within me. Through many interactions and reflections, I have expanded the first ideas in new directions while remaining deeply rooted in the principles of education I seek to embody in my pedagogical praxis. The goal to write about a *Pedagogy for a Planetary Convivência* (Planetary Conviviality)[1] in the context of religious education is a challenging task, and I know I write from a specific context that is historically, socially, politically, and religiously located, with its own ideology, but also from a passionate heartfelt commitment and urgency. Precisely because of this, I do not claim to understand or speak for all contexts or people. My attempt is, however, to broaden the conversation and to call attention to this relevant theme in the current crisis of hopelessness and exhaustion in which human beings and the planet are immersed.

Religious formation has been crucial in forming human communities as a means of continuity, passing down cultural, moral, and spiritual values across generations, even though history teaches us that religious institutions are not beyond betrayal of the very values and morals they preach. Religious education has become increasingly complex in the face of urgent global challenges that demand an active stance towards promoting social

---

1. I intentionally chose the Portuguese word *convivência* instead of conviviality. Later in the book I will explain the reasons for doing so.

Introduction

justice, equity, and lasting social transformation. In the context of theological education—especially in seminaries aimed at ministerial formation, whether focused on traditional or non-traditional models of ministry—the theme of global relationships has gained attention not only from specific disciplines but also across initiatives that seek to transcend the ecclesial and cultural boundaries by raising awareness about the interconnectedness we all experience as humans in a globalized world. Not surprisingly, many schools have taken interest in providing local spaces where intercultural immersion can occur or in offering travel experiences aiming to educate their students to become aware and more sophisticated in their analyses of *glocal* interconnections. However, we should be cautious since these added-on curriculum items may not necessarily change the DNA of colonialism, racism, and sexism that are still present in religious education through both omission or commission. Today, most cross-cultural efforts in theological education aim to teach students to learn from others in contexts other than their local and familiar settings. It is hoped that exposure to other forms of living and interactions with different cultures and territories would allow students to expand their understanding of others and foster a new, more amicable, if not humane, way to live and interact with others.

Many people have attempted to break free from the colonial mindset of believing they are the sole possessors of knowledge, a gift from God, and constantly teaching others without being open to learning from them. Unfortunately, this paternalistic objective has, by and large, failed in view of the spiritual values and moral religious education is charged to teach. Overcoming this generalized failure involves avoiding preconceived notions that limit our ability to perceive and understand others. At the same time we must be receptive to what others can teach us about ourselves. As Mikhail Bakhtin appropriately put it that, as humans, we gain knowledge about ourselves from others as a "surplus of vision."[2] The term surplus vision refers to what we see and shape from our respective positions. Consciousness arises from otherness and from this excess of seeing in relation to the other. Individuals have a "surplus" or excess of vision in relation to the other, according to Bakhtin, to the extent that they are able to perceive what the other cannot see and vice versa. We are all unique, but we are also incomplete without each other. The isolated individual cannot be fully aware of him or herself. We need other people to reveal to us things about ourselves that otherwise will not be known. As difficult as it is to admit,

---

2. Holquist, *Dialogism: Bakhtin and His World*, 36–37.

recognizing otherness (outwardness) implies recognizing our interdependence and accepting that, individually, we are limited, and we need others to overcome our mutual incompleteness. In Freire's writings we find the notion of conscientization, which encompasses not only the recognition of others and what they reveal about us and our own unfinishedness, but also the idea that this process entails the awareness of the reality that surrounds us. The diversity of our experiences should offer us opportunities for mutually enhancing creative activities and strengthening our values and behaviors. However, contexts, beliefs, and traditions are never neutral. They are always shaped by how we embrace them as we engage in praxis in our quotidian relationships. Sometimes, the openness toward cultural and global exchanges can reveal potential conflictive relationships in the insatiable quest for power and control through which new forms of colonialism are engendered through institutions, particularly schooling. Social, cultural, and historical contexts also inform and influence theological reflections since these reflections cannot escape the very ideology that shapes them. Religious institutions can either become a part of the colonial machine by staying silent in the face of growing hatred, selfishness, cruelty, racism, individualism and self-serving spiritual formulas, or they can engage in decolonial approaches. These decolonial approaches should be formed in ethics and resistance, and should aim to identify and disrupt global processes that perpetuate the colonial legacies of violence that we are witnessing worldwide.

Although we recognize the central role that establishment education plays in preparing individuals to understand and address complex global dynamics, we also recognize how rarely establishment education has challenged the prevailing assumptions of dominant groups or confronted the myths and distortions of their worldviews. As a result, establishment education, which is too often acritical, has validated egregious policies, omitted different perspectives, and discouraged civic engagement as it perpetuates a White male narrative which is, by definition, exclusionary of women and nonwhites. Whether the context is religious or non-religious, the central role that education plays is usually unquestionable and requires a critical approach to dismantle and decolonize previous forms of understanding our mutual dependence and responsibility. As Freire reminds us, education cannot do everything, but it can foster the critical reflection on, and openness to, understanding social structures that perpetuate dominance

Introduction

and violence,[3] helping us to recognize how what is happening locally affects other people globally and the planet. Hence an emancipatory education as proposed by Freire can educate people to be self-conscious so that, even as an ordinary citizen, one can and should contribute to and actively participate in creating a more humane and sustainable world where all can flourish. It can help us critically to appraise how communal efforts can forge inclusive and liberating sites for living and thriving as a collective whose *raison d'etre* is social justice.

Bounded by the increasing deterioration of the earth's resources and hostile human relationships, education and its agents are charged with the task of recuperating and recalibrating social interactions in ways that promote coexistence that is less self-centered and more other-centered. Grounded on the recognition of the interdependence and interconnectedness between that which is local yet global, between people and environment, and between action and consequences, this book represents one praxis among many others. Although I speak from my experience, I hope the reader can connect and relate to many themes herewith presented. The content of this book is born out of my passion and concern about human endeavors and relationships, and it is from my location and positionality as a Christian Brazilian woman that I feel compelled to write as a form of participation in the greater cause of global social justice. I do not intend to convey a comprehensive understanding of what global interconnections entail or grasp all the complexities of the ecological crisis we are facing. I aim to make some initial suggestions and offer insights into the compounding effects of colonialism and imperialism on our current crisis. I approach this with tender energy that first invites me to resist and overcome any fear or sense of inadequacy.

I am cognizant that my writing is risky because I choose to write with "an accent," drawing from theologies and epistemologies of the Global South. Furthermore, I am not hiding where I come from (Brazil), nor my religious background (Christian) which I indicated earlier, nor which epistemological locus I inhabit (critical educator). In my effort to share my thoughts, I recognize that my writing is a form of re-existence—others would probably say survival.[4] It is an attempt to share the collective wisdom of many voices that, under different circumstances and contexts, have been rendered *inaudible*. Because of that, I do not dare to walk alone on this

---

3. Freire, *Educação como Prática da Liberdade*, 24.
4. Walsh, *Pedagogías Decoloniales*, 2–68.

journey. On the contrary, I walk in the company of other sojourners who have paved the way before me. They continue to inspire and invite me to embrace a kind of solidarity capable of overcoming centuries of patriarchy, imperialism, colonialism, xenophobia, and homophobia, among many other "isms" that try to divide us and to make any collaborative effort worthless. Also, I walk along with many theological partners who have shared their insights, struggles, and joys in the often dry and lonely corridors of academia but who, in subtle and creative ways, have defied the individualistic arrangements and systems through which we must maneuver to construct not only a theology *en conjunto* but a *pedagogy for convivência*.[5]

Despite carving a way of togetherness, I own my mistakes and shortcomings about what is expressed here in the hope that you, the reader, fill in the blanks, add your stories, critique the points of limitations, and include your perception about the world we inhabit. Writing from a Freirean approach, I have no intention or desire to provide a recipe or manual on how to shape this path. On the contrary, I expect to offer some dialogue starters, some questions to ponder and to describe the pathway I have taken as I continue to journey seeking a better *convivência* on this planet. The rise of conflicting relationships because of political, economic, ethnic, religious, and cultural disputes reveals the urgent need to educate for a planetary *convivência* that encompasses all aspects of our lives. It is impossible to think about *convivência* only among those with whom we have some sort of relationship through family ties, work, communal or social bonds. There is a much greater urgency in learning how we can or should relate with one another in ways that respect and recognize our differences and the sacredness of life in every human and non-human being.

Although we know this goal, we need a collective effort along many different fronts. As educators, we believe in the centrality of education to help us in this endeavor. Indeed, the educational principles required to undertake this task cannot dismiss the challenges and the urgencies of communities living through these critical times and how communal efforts can create inclusive and liberating sites where we can live and thrive. I believe that Paulo Freire's extensive body of work can offer theoretical and pedagogical insights that speak specifically to the social, political, cultural, and environmental dilemmas we are facing today. Throughout his pilgrimage, he never walked alone. He had intellectual partners journeying with him and a community

---

5. Later the word will be explained in detail. It suffices to say that the word connotes the idea of "living with." This word will recur in different parts of the text.

Introduction

of teachers-learners dialoguing with him to help expand his insights. I am not walking alone either. I write inspired and *alargada* (enlarged) by my continuous *travessias* (crossings) and dialogues with different authors and colleagues in the Americas with whom I have shared my journey.

During my *travessias,* I have crossed many geographical, cultural, and religious borders. From these experiences, I came to understand that it is impossible to traverse these borders without being *atravessada* (crossed), as Gloria Anzaldua poignantly describes the feeling of being crossed. For many, crossing borders is a challenging and intimidating experience, and for her it felt like returning to *una herida abierta*,[6] an open wound. Although most of the time this crisscrossing is painful, the exercise of crossing borders allows a person to develop an expanded perception of reality and to understand the political articulations to which she is subjected to, as well as to recognize her multiple identities. This exercise, as Anzaldua, vividly describes, also allows the breaking of dualisms, binary oppositions, and generates an identity of frontier which she calls a borderland identity or a mestiza consciousness: "The work of mestiza consciousness is to break down the subject-object duality that keeps her a prisoner and to show in the flesh and through the images in her work how duality is transcended."[7] Therefore, borderland identity grants the ability to crossover different cultures to acquire tolerance for ambiguities and to develop a kind of resilience capable of transforming pain and frustration into an experience of confidence and groundedness.

In Portuguese, there is another meaning to this word, *atravessada*.[8] It refers to someone who violates conventional norms of etiquette. A person who might be perceived as inconvenient, unsuitable, or undesirable. I bring the meaning of this word in both languages to recognize its polyvalence and to affirm the importance of considering both meanings. Thus, *atravessada* here constitutes a profound awareness of one's condition as oppressed and an intense sense of resistance and resilience. A traversed person not only carries an *herida abierta* that cuts through her soul, but she also bears in her innermost being the resilience that gives her the strength to refuse being submitted to the prescribed forms of behavior and expectations that

---

6. Anzaldúa, *Borderlands/La Frontera*, 25.

7. Anzaldúa, *Borderlands/La Frontera*, 102.

8. The word in Portuguese, spelled *atravessada*, is especially used in the Northeast region of Brazil, my birthplace, to refer to someone who does not behave properly, and who inadvertently becomes inconvenient.

try to colonize her actions and her existence. Being *atravessada* constitutes a defiant and resilient position, a site that evokes a "spirit of survivance," a term coined by Anishinaabe literary theorist Gerald Vizenor. He describes survivance as an active presence beyond mere survival that encompasses resistance. This compelling concept conveys a "renunciation of dominance, tragedy, and victimry."[9] Instead of accommodating to a position of being oppressed, one resists it. However, this resistance comes not from a place of victimization but from a place of agency. I am enriched by Vizenor's understanding of survivance because it helps me to realize that our *travessias* are always a mixture of survival and resistance as we try to navigate turbulent waters of oppression, sometimes totally submerged and other times fighting back to grab the air above.

Experiences of crossing are constant reminders of our otherness, and the perennial effort to resist any attempt to dehumanize who we are. They constitute pathways on which we can educate the eyes and the memories of our hearts to embrace humanizing experiences that embody civility, honesty, cooperation, generosity, and respect for differences. The education of our eyes and how we perceive one another is essential in these times, given the deteriorating crisis of values at the core of contemporary societies. We all need new perspectives to react to the harsh reality in which we live and re-exist.

From my transcultural experiences in Brazil, Argentina, the United States, or in any other countries I have visited, I carry concrete experiences and fond memories of people, places, and their unique ways of expressing themselves. For instance, sharing the "mate" in Argentina was not just drinking a kind of tea but taking part in a ritual of friendship that would bring me a sense of community, of belonging, and an opportunity to experience an ancestral gift from the Guaranis, original people of South America. Visiting Peru, I learned the meaning of the word *Qonakuy*, "I bring the best of me myself to the encounter with you," which embodies a true practice of hospitality.[10] I learned from Hawaiians that "Aloha" is more than a greeting; it is a form of living and expression encompassing feelings of love, affection, kindness, and goodness deeply rooted in Hawaiian culture. In New Zealand, I learned the expression *Kia Ora*, in the Māori language, which means "Have life" or "Be healthy," and the "Hongi—the sharing of breath"

---

9. Vizenor, *Manifest Manners*, vii.

10. The word *Qonakuy* was shared during the biannual meeting on missions of the Methodist Church of Peru, held in the Peruvian capital in 2018.

Introduction

performed during special occasions, a sacred act in which two people press their noses against each other, a tradition in which the visitor becomes unified with those performing the hongi ritual. Those who partake in the ritual become responsible for respecting the land and its natural gifts of beauty.

Growing up in Brazilian culture, I learned the importance of hugs. It was second nature for me to express physical affection toward family and friends. Hugs are more than just a gesture of closeness or acceptance. The fundamental element of a hug is that there is no embrace without the presence of the other. These experiences have enriched me deeply and rooted within me a profound appreciation for the multicolored and multifaced aspects of these cultures. They have broadened my vision and have made me an expansive version of myself. Because of these life experiences, I have developed a particular interest on the topic of intercultural relations and the challenges they bring forth, especially when there is a significant increase in diversity regarding not only race, ethnicity, culture, nationality, but also diversity of ideological convictions, religious beliefs, and practices. My personal story has been woven into a larger patchwork of multiple stories. They are not static or fixed in time, but they are circular, always evolving out of differences and commonalities that I have encountered throughout the experiences I undergo as pilgrim on this earth, always crossing and being crossed.

While the term *atravessada* usually refers to a person being crossed, I imagine that the land, as a living being, has also been crossed over. The land has been traversed in a painful way without regard to her rivers, forests, and ecosystems. As a living being, it has witnessed the path of destruction scattering in all directions. The earth, our first womb, the living being that embraced us into its home, suffers the consequences of human action drastically and irreparably. Yet, Pachamama continues to shower us with generosity and exuberance in ways that take our breath away. How can one not come to a complete stop when contemplating a sunset captured in awe? Facing the majesty of a forest, the exuberance of rivers, or the immensity of the sea? Or the winds, textures, and changing colors of each season?

On my travels to and from my country of residence to my country of birth, I always experience a spiritual connection with the land that welcomes me. Even when the people who inhabit these places are unaware of my arrival or departure, the motherland always embraces, holds, and welcomes me. In these moments, I feel an almost palpable emotion of ancestral connection that gives me back the nectar of life and the realization of belonging. The earth reenergizes me, restores my body, heals my soul, and connects my spirit. This is why I like to imagine that I belong to many places and that the earth always welcomes me wherever my feet touch it. I also like to imagine that my family is expansive; I have many brothers and sisters scattered around the world. According to ancient wisdom, we are all interconnected in a big family that includes not only humans but also rivers, forests, mountains, and more. To restore our relationship and connectivity to Earth, we must let that visceral connection guide our paths toward a more conscious existence, recognizing that we inhabit these intersections of Earth, human and non-human beings. That's why we need to walk this land gently.

I also want to consider how we are marking and traversing Mother Earth with our footprints, which have historically been heavy, careless, and hurtful. When I was a doctoral student, one of my professors gave me a mug that I continue to carry with me and which I intentionally keep in front of my books as a reminder of the Indian blessing imprinted that says, "Let's walk softly on this earth with all living beings, great and small, remembering as we go, that one God, kind and wise, created all." I believe this is the ancestral wisdom that we need to recover in our daily lives. From this place of reflection, I want to offer some insights into the need we have as a planetary community to re-educate our minds, bodies, and spirits for a loving experience with people and everything that exists. Simply put, a planetary community and war are mutually exclusive. Hence, this humble book seeks to urge my fellow human beings to imagine a world where humans can finally understand the greatness of belonging, rather than the desire to possess and control. Instead of accumulating material goods, we will be sharing gestures and affections, the true concrete achievements of our humanity, not as an aspiration, but as a concrete reality. To walk gently on the earth is to learn from it; it means not remaining indifferent or neutral but engaging with all human and more-than-human, recognizing how all the ecosystems relate to one another in an organic and dependent way.

Overview of the Chapters

In Chapter 1, we take a deep dive into the core of educational practices, unraveling the intricate interplay between cognitive development and emotional intelligence. "The Heart of Education and the Education of the Heart" calls on educators and learners to acknowledge the value of

Introduction

developing the brain and heart. Here, we explore the idea that, in addition to academic proficiency, a holistic approach to education should foster the growth of emotional resilience, empathy, and ethical awareness.

The chapter contends that proper education entails more than just learning facts. Therefore, educators may build environments that develop compassion, a feeling of connectivity, and intellectual curiosity by acknowledging and embracing the emotional elements of learning. A healthy heart improves cognitive function and adds to the general well-being of the person and the community, demonstrating the mutual relationship between the heart and education.

In essence, this chapter guides us toward an educational paradigm that cherishes the symbiosis between emotional knowledge and intellectual rigor. It lays the groundwork for a transformative educational experience that enriches the mind and nurtures the very core of our humanity—the heart. As we delve deeper into the subsequent chapters, we carry with us the profound understanding that the heart of education beats in unison with the education of the heart.

Chapter 2 provides an overarching idea for creating a pedagogy that emphasizes planetary *convivência*, that is, a compelling vision for humanity that transcends conventional notions of development and progress. Central to this chapter are the concepts of *convivência* and *buen vivir*. The word *convivência*, which translates to conviviality, refers to the quality of social relations that promote friendship, community, and a sense of belonging. It means the ability of different cultures to live together. The chapter explores the importance of conviviality and its importance in education, showing how this concept is crucial for any educational process, both conceptually and practically. I used the word cognate in Portuguese, *convivência*, to highlight the implied meanings that the Portuguese word bears.

The expression *buen vivir*, which translates to "good living" or "living well," aims to shed light on the crucial aspects of the ancestral cosmovision of the indigenous people of Latin America, through the perspective of Guarani People. *Buen vivir* emphasizes the interconnectedness, reciprocity, and reverence for nature, recognizing that human well-being is intricately linked to the well-being of the Earth and its diverse ecosystems. In essence, *buen vivir* fosters a profound sense of ecological citizenship, where humans perceive themselves as integral parts of the natural world rather than its masters. Unlike the prevailing Western model of development, which often prioritizes economic growth at the expense of environmental degradation and social inequality, *buen vivir* advocates for a holistic approach to life that integrates spiritual, ecological, and communal dimensions.

At its heart, *Buen Vivir* Towards a Planetary *Convivência* chapter challenges the prevailing paradigm of anthropocentrism, which views nature merely as a resource to be exploited for human benefit. Instead, it champions a relational ontology that acknowledges the intrinsic value of all life forms and seeks to cultivate reciprocal relationships based on respect, empathy, and solidarity. Ultimately, the chapter invites us to envision a more just and equitable world where indigenous people are honored as stewards of the land, cultural diversity is celebrated and respected, and relationships between humans and the natural world are characterized by reciprocity and care.

In Chapter 3, we delve into the multifaceted dimensions of education, exploring how it can serve as a powerful catalyst for social change. Whether in rural villages, remote cities, or metropolises, we are in constant contact with different cultures, traditions, and ways of being. These places function as political and social activity centers, allowing us to engage in city life and fulfill our civic duties. However, interactions in these contact zones can occasionally lead to conflict, animosity, and injustice, especially when democracies around the world are under attack with the rise of political extremism and religious fundamentalism.

Social Responsibility for Planetary *Convivência* chapter highlights the significance of reflecting on the fact that democracy cannot exist or be maintained without informed and critically engaged citizens. The fundamental role of critical education, as opposed to education-for-profit, is to educate critical citizens. By acknowledging the role of liberating education in shaping critical citizens, the chapter emphasizes a broader understanding of our responsibilities as planetary citizens. It underlines the importance of not only forming such critical citizens but also empathetic and respectful individuals to build a coexistence that values human dignity and works for the common good.

Chapter 4, Care-Full Education: Resisting a Culture of Care-Less-ness, constitutes a call to action in a world where detachment and apathy are increasingly prevalent. Building on the previous chapter's critique of contemporary educational systems that prioritize efficiency and performance metrics over the holistic development of students as empathetic and compassionate beings, this chapter highlights the importance of care. It suggests that questioning why particular lives are considered more valuable than others can help us better understand human relationships more compassionately.

The core of *care-full* education is centered around the idea of cultivating inclusive and supportive learning spaces where students feel acknowledged, listened to, and appreciated. It opposes the belief that education is a mechanical process and instead adopts pedagogies of care that prioritize building relationships, trust, and cooperation. In this paradigm, teachers become mentors and facilitators of growth, guiding students on a journey of self-discovery and ethical reflection. The chapter also explores care from a spiritual perspective, providing examples of how Jesus, in his practice, embodied a pedagogy of care that mercifully cared for those forgotten and marginalized by society. Thus, it reminds us that education is not a neutral enterprise but a transformative force capable of reshaping individual consciousness and promoting collective action. By embracing a culture of care, compassion, and social responsibility, we can resist the prevailing culture of carelessness and create a more just, equitable, and empathetic society for all.

Evoking the wisdom of rivers that, when facing obstacles in their current flow, find new paths to move forward, Principles to *Sulear* our *Convivência* Pedagogy chapter deepens this metaphor, inviting us to give vent to the flow of life and our educational efforts with creativity and openness. Instead of a pedagogy of cruelty, the chapter proposes a pedagogy guided by principles that foster planetary coexistence. Based on Freire's ideas about literacy as a political and liberatory process and his ideas about generative words, the chapter suggests a similar process to ground the praxis of the pedagogy for planetary *convivência*.

In Freire's conception, the process of generative words is not static. It is derived from everyday experiences, leading to syntheses about sociocultural reality. This dynamic process is open to modifications and expansions, constantly evolving due to its creative and contextual potential. For Freire, generative words cannot be separated from life and political struggle, relationships of affection or knowledge constructed together. Therefore, the chapter 5 suggests Hope, Lovingness, Dialogue, and Solidarity as educational principles that can serve as the foundation of the Pedagogy for Planetary *Convivência*. These principles are not intended to be an end in themselves but rather a starting point that encourages the exploration of broader themes and circles of belonging.

The last chapter may seem overly idealistic and utopian. However, I present it not as a final product, but as a work in progress. My intention is not to provide a recipe, but to identify and suggest some pathways so that we can reconstruct our pedagogies otherwise. Pedagogy Otherwise: Cartography of Affection chapter takes us on a deep dive into the maze of human emotions and relationships, transcending mere exploration to unveil the transformative power inherent in understanding and navigating the intricate terrain of our interconnected affections. At its essence, the chapter claims that our emotional landscape is a rich quilt woven from the threads of our experiences, memories, and interactions with others. Through taking a cartographical journey, we want to explore the boundaries of our inner selves and find the undiscovered routes that profoundly and meaningfully unite us.

Central to this exploration is the recognition that emotions are not isolated phenomena but dynamic forces that shape our perceptions, actions, and relationships. By charting the landscape of our emotions, we may gain insight into the complex interplay of love, joy, grief, rage, and fear that shape our lived experiences. As we navigate the contours of our emotional landscapes, we appreciate the shared humanity that binds us, transcending the boundaries of culture, language, and ideology. In an increasingly divided society, we may make genuine connections, develop a sense of belonging, and establish deeper connections by embracing the complexity and diversity of human emotions. In essence, this chapter becomes a roadmap that enables us to traverse the intricacies of the human experience with compassion, grace, and perseverance. By charting our emotional landscapes with intention and mindfulness, we unlock the potential for healing, growth, and connection, forging pathways toward a more empathetic, inclusive, and compassionate society for all.

1

The Heart of Education and the Education of the Heart

> "Human beings are not born once and for all on the day their mothers give birth to them, but ... life obliges them over and over again to give birth to themselves."
>
> —Gabriel García Márquez, *Love in the Time of Cholera*

INFORMED BY THE WORK of Paulo Freire[1] and the pedagogies and theologies of the South, I share the concerns of many who have identified the impact of globalization on the environment and the lives of the most vulnerable individuals, who are directly or indirectly forced to sacrifice their humanity to appease the whims of a select few. Looking at these dynamics from a critical education perspective, it's clear to see how the process of colonization has had a significant impact on education and continues to do so. It's undeniable that education has reinforced liberal discourses and unfair economic policies that prioritize technological rationality over

---

1. Paulo Freire, patron of Brazilian education, is one of the most notable intellectuals of the 20th century—who crossed geographic and linguistic boundaries—and continues to inspire educators around the world with his vision of education as an act of love and courage. He is most known by his book, *Pedagogy of the Oppressed* which has been translated to more than 40 languages. See https://ilas.columbia.edu/freireinitiative.

human necessities. Many educational institutions have shifted their focus towards achieving outcomes and generating profits, rather than prioritizing teaching and learning that aims to bring about positive transformations. Meanwhile, liberal discourses tend to be designed in a way that encourages individuals to conform to the pre-existing reality constructed by those holding positions of power.

As critical educators, it is our duty to seek to cultivate alternative ways to live our lives and to relate to one another in fair, just, compassionate, respectful, and dignified ways. From an educational outlook, these predicaments and interferences cannot be solved only by implementing new policies or creating an inclusive curriculum without changing the very structures that perpetuate exploitation and dehumanization of individuals who lack power to claim their agency. As to Paulo Freire reminds us, "in the last analysis the basic presupposition of such action is the illusion that the hearts of men and women can be transformed while the social structures that make those hearts 'sick' are left intact and unchanged."[2] Therefore, when we do not seek to resolve the causes of inequalities and social exclusion, which create both victims and oppressors, nothing effectively changes. Even when we sometimes try to resolve the animosity between victims and perpetrators by convincing them to tolerate and reconcile their differences, we have not worked hard enough to solve the vicious and violent systems that produce both victims and perpetrators, as well as the cruel circumstances which give rise to oppressive conditions.

From my perspective, education cannot be effective if it is not concerned with educating the heart, for, as Parker Palmer, world-renowned writer, speaker, and activist asserts, "the heart is the place where intellect and emotion and spirit and will converge in the human self."[3] Oftentimes, we get used to ignoring our intuition and prefer to follow imposed rules of etiquette or academic obligations, to seek supposed professional achievements, and to follow the prescription of what knowledge is and how we should acquire it. Thus, we act less with the heart and body, allowing ourselves to be governed by the imposition of the outer worlds. Hostage to these socially constructed demands, we become "knowledgeable in the head" and not "wise in the heart." Data storage in our intellect becomes more important than the wisdom that must be born in our hearts, the wisdom capable of germinating life and producing transformation. When emotions are absent

---

2. Freire, *The Politics of Education*, 122.
3. Palmer, *The Courage to Teach*, 11.

The Heart of Education and the Education of the Heart

in the educational process, as Antonia Darder, critical educator and activist, contends, "the result is often scholarship conceived epistemologically in a deeply estranged way, devoid of the very qualities that compromise our humanity."[4] Such disembodied knowledge rarely results in a more critical analysis of deeper educational problems, let alone in a challenge to the social and material relations that underpin human suffering and structural inequalities. There is, therefore, a need to develop new ways of learning and new sensitivities to improve the way we relate to others and our planet. From this place, we can prioritize genuine care and concern for everything that constitutes, and can make, our coexistence possible.

Boaventura de Sousa Santos, a sociologist and legal scholar regarded as one of the most prominent Portuguese living intellectuals, in his book *The End of Cognitive Empire*, explains a captivating expression shared among the native Pueblos of Central and South America, *corazonar*,[5] meaning "to warm up the heart" where reason and emotions fuse. *Corazonar*, an expression that represents both kind-heartedness and resistance, emerges from the struggles of indigenous and Afro-descendants' peoples of Latin America. For them, *corazonar* is a spiritual and political stance, an insurgent energy against oppression. It is an expanded way of *being-with* that increases reciprocity and communion that does not fit the conventional dichotomies mind/body, private/public, individual/collective, says Santos. I believe that this important experience, which has been practiced by the indigenous people since forever, should be cultivated in each of us. *Corazonar* is nothing more than the ability to allow the heart to guide our reason and emotion, and making possible, as Freire envisions, "the creation of a world in which it will be easier to love."[6] This vital energy would certainly impel us toward solidarity, coexistence, and resistance.

Karen Baker-Fletcher insightfully suggests that "our task is to grow large hearts, large minds, reconnecting with earth, Spirit, and one another,"[7] which echoes the apostle Paul when he counsels the Corinthians, asking them to open their hearts wide. Paul writes: "We have spoken freely to you, Corinthians, and opened wide our hearts to you. We are not withholding our affection from you, but you are withholding yours from us. As a fair exchange—I speak as to my children—open wide your hearts also." (2 Cor 6:11–13).

4. Darder, *Freire and Education*, 78.
5. Sousa Santos, *The End of Cognitive Empire*, 99–101.
6. Freire, *The Pedagogy of the Oppressed*, 19.
7. Baker-Fletcher, *Sisters of Dust, Sisters of Spirit*, 93.

A Pedagogy for Planetary *Convivência*

As children of savage capitalism, we have bowed to the impositions of the neoliberal system that sucks our blood, consumes our energies, and shrinks our hearts so that, anesthetized, we do not feel the pain and the effects of losing our humanity. Having our eyes dazzled by the glittering lights of *having more,* we forget to *be more.* Sometimes, because of the hectic pace of life, we would rather conform to prescribed and imposed discourse than take the time or guts to develop new worldviews that are more in line with what our senses are able to see, feel, and understand. We forget that we are beings of connection, integrated into an organism larger than ourselves. Everything that separates us from ourselves, from others, from the earth, and from the Creator, dehumanizes us and objectifies us. As Jewish theologian and activist Abraham Joshua Heschel acutely recognizes, "education has failed to educate hearts and minds not taking seriously the need of love to mobilize and articulate the 'heart, intelligence and wealth for the purpose of love and justice.'"[8] As a result of educational failure, we have a system that prepares professionals to master the world of external reality to manage new technologies and advancements but not to be able to address the deeper issues of our inward world. As Palmer accurately summarizes, "We train doctors to repair the body but not to honor the spirit; clergy to be CEO but not spiritual guides; teachers to master techniques but not to engage their students' souls."[9] Consequently, education has focused mainly on educating the intellect, thus restricting our ability to explore, understand, and connect our lives, other people, and the cosmos more deeply. The prevailing paradigm focuses on knowledge, skills, and material acquisitions that neglect the meaning and purpose of life. This creates a massive void for students and educators alike, resulting in frustration, disconnection, and unhappiness.

The heart is a muscular organ that, through its contraction and expansion, ensures that nutrients and oxygen reach every cell in the body. It is the cord—the word heart comes from the Latin word, *cordis*—the common thread that connects our organs and the vital functions of the body. For many, it is the center of the soul, intelligence, and sensitivity. The human heart is both fragility and strength. It can be vulnerable but also strong, bearing the world's pain. With it, we can love but also hate. Or, as Parker Palmer says, the heart "is the center place where all of our ways of knowing converge—intellectual, emotional, sensory, intuitive, imaginative,

---

8. Heschel, *The Insecurity of Freedom,* 59.
9. Palmer, *The Courage to Teach,* 19.

experiential, relational, and bodily, among others."[10] As I contemplate the significance of the heart, I cannot help but wonder why we tend to neglect the centrality of *corazonar* in our education endeavors. What type of education would enable us to expand our hearts rather than constrict them?

In his sensitive book *Los Derechos del Corazón* (*The Rights of the Heart*), Leonardo Boff, considered one of the fathers of Liberation Theology, reminds us, "the heart has its own rights and its own logic. It doesn't see as clearly as reason, but it looks in deeper and more accurate ways. We know better when we love. And we love more intensely when our knowledge is more lucid and less prejudiced."[11] He advises that if we do not rescue our sensitive reason, which is an essential dimension of the soul, it will be difficult for us to begin to respect the otherness of beings, to love Mother Earth with all her ecosystems, and to live compassionately toward those who suffer in nature and humanity.

If reason counts profits and losses, the heart is what teaches us to multiply our hopes and share our cares. When deprived of our sensitive and cordial intelligence, we open the door for the insanity and greed that have led to terrible crimes committed throughout human history against individuals, communities, and entire populations, such as the recent case that the Yanomami people in Brazil suffered during Covid-19 due to government indifference and the greed of miners. Not only did they suffer the consequences of the pandemic, but they suffered also greatly from disease and starvation. Analysts attribute this catastrophe to the large number of illegal miners who have taken up camp in their vast territory because of the greed of those searching for gold.[12] Fiona Watson, research and advocacy director at indigenous human rights group Survival International, said high malaria rates—spread by miners—have left many Yanomami adults too unwell to hunt or fish, as they rely entirely on the forest and rivers for food.[13] As Brazilian neuroscientist Sidarta Ribeiro argues, dependence on the accumulation of money, objects, and experiences leads to a consumerist epidemic that devours the environment and devastates the mind. According

---

10. Palmer, *Healing the Heart of Democracy*, 6.

11. Boff, *Los derechos del corazón*, 10.

12. As of June 30, 2021, 163 different indigenous peoples had been infected by Covid-19, totaling 5,6174 infected people, of which 1,126 died. The lethality rate among indigenous people was almost double that found in the Brazilian population in general. See Ribeiro, *Sonho Manifesto*, 38.

13. See https://www.cnn.com/2023/02/11/americas/brazil-yanomami-mining-crackdown-intl-latam/index.html

to him, we live in "a painful, contagious, and socially transmitted condition of overload, debt, anxiety, and waste, resulting from the single-minded pursuit of having more."[14] The future cannot be sustained at the current rate; thus, humanity needs to find a new path that comes from the heart rather than the wallet.

Boff calls attention to the centrality of the heart as a structuring axis of social organization and offers a fine example of cordiality found in the Nahuatl culture of the Aztecs of Mexico. He says that the Nahuatl people attributed great significance to the heart. To them, a human being was not merely a thinking creature but rather an individual with a unique identity and emotional center. The face was the distinguishing feature that set one person apart from another, and encountering another person elicited a sense of ethical responsibility, as philosopher Emmanuel Lévinas has taught us. The face reveals whether we welcome, embrace, distrust, or disregard someone, but it is the heart that "defines the way of being and the character of the person, the sensitivity towards the other, the cordial welcome and the compassion towards the one who suffers."[15] As Boff confirms, the refined education of the Aztecs, preserved in deeply beautiful texts, sought to form in young people a "clear, kind and shadowless face" combined to a "firm and warm heart, determined and hospitable, supportive and respectful of sacred things."[16]

Restoring the cordial reason requires cooperation rather than individual effort. In these dire times, educating the heart is essential because, frequently, when the severity of living conditions is disregarded, the heart becomes more rigid, and impulses toward cruelty become more pervasive. Evil can thrive if one's conscience is sick enough to let it. It seems improbable that such awareness—or rather, its absence—could sense another person's suffering. To satisfy its craving for power, a damaged conscience may also attempt to objectify people by deceptive deeds, which are occasionally covered up by comforting statements and false words. These qualities are not set in stone, as they are learned through socialization. Education that emphasizes the beauty of the human spirit has the ability to transform them. Freire believes that when the mind and heart are aligned, we can witness "testimonies of the gratuitous loving of life."[17] By achieving this unity,

14. Ribeiro, *Sonho Manifesto*, 18.
15. Boff, *Los derechos del corazón*, 67.
16. Boff, *Los derechos del corazón*, 67.
17. Freire, *Pedagogy of Indignation*, 103.

we are merging conflicting ideas and establishing a foundation for a more empathetic praxis.

The concept of praxis for Freire is centered around the interaction between individuals and their relationship with the world around them. Genuine communication, according to Freire, is built upon love, respect for diversity, and a belief in equal relationships between people. This approach aims to counteract the hierarchical nature of banking education[18] by promoting dialogue that empowers individuals and can be facilitated through circles of conversations, or circles of culture as Freire used to call them. In this way, education becomes a collaborative effort where everyone is both a learner and a teacher, working together toward a common goal. To achieve this, educators must prioritize fostering a welcoming and horizontal relationship with their students, laying a model and the foundation for a truly democratic society.

In addition, education can facilitate the transformation of persons into responsible individuals who hold themselves, others, and creation in high regard. Instead of being solely motivated by self-interest, individuals can develop a sense of compassion, love, and humility as they strive for the betterment of humanity. Society often emphasizes the importance of material possessions, but true fulfillment and connection can only be achieved by considering the needs of others, the environment, and the recognition of the divine in our daily experiences. Our hearts are responsible for keeping us alive, and if they fail, we cannot resist, much less yet exist.

In today's world, where we see widespread efforts to suppress critical thinking, undermine democratic processes, and perpetuate violence against vulnerable members of our communities, the ideas of Freire remain relevant. Freire was influenced by writers like Frantz Fanon and Albert Memmi,[19] who fought against colonialism and worked to improve the lives of those considered the "wretched of the earth." Freire's decolonial thought emphasizes the importance of valuing the knowledge and experiences of oppressed groups instead of disregarding them as the dominant discourse often does. Freire's lifelong dedication to ethics provides insights into

---

18. Freire, *Pedagogy of the Oppressed*, 52–57.

19. In the 1970s, Freire helped several countries of the African continent during the process of political emancipation from European colonization, which aimed above all at valuing the culture, history, and local experiences of the African peoples. During this period, he became more familiar with Amilcar Cabral's work and began to nurture great admiration for him.

A Pedagogy for Planetary *Convivência*

navigating the current planetary crisis and the importance of maintaining hope for a better society.

The insightful notion that "reading the world" ought to come before "reading the word" applies to the ideas presented in this book.[20] Similar to how the prophets of Judeo-Christian tradition exhort us to "read the signs of the times," we are asked to understand the current age (Matthew 16:3, NSRV). The "limit-situations"[21] that humanity and the planet face require analysis and reflection that leads to conscientization, as Freire calls it, which must be anchored in praxis. Conscientization refers to a deliberate effort to attain freedom through conscious action and a critical approach to uncovering the truth. As oppression stems from the dominance of specific systems, it is crucial thoroughly to analyze all aspects of this process and collaborate to find solutions. Freire suggests that critical thinking is integral in this process, allowing people to recognize the institutional powers that create divides and sustain exclusion. Additionally, Freire stresses that critical thinking should be rooted in an ethical obligation to transform the pernicious circumstances that individuals encounter. Consequently, he regards conscientization as a process that frees both the oppressed and the oppressor and can bring about liberation.

Though we understand that education plays a crucial role in helping people understand and respond to the complexities of our world, we also acknowledge that education designed by the dominant class often fails to challenge the myths and distortions of dominant groups' perspectives. Such failure has led to unjust and discriminatory policies, the suppression of opposing views, and has decreased civic engagement. Religious education, more specifically, runs the risk of perpetuating such behaviors and neglecting its responsibility to promote societal and individual transformation. To promote justice and harmony, religious education must recognize the interconnectedness of all things and teach social responsibility that respects our interconnectedness. This includes educating individuals and communities on planetary awareness and fostering a commitment to respecting God and neighbors while caring for our shared world-home.

Unfortunately, many religious communities seem to have forgotten the fundamental principles of our shared humanity, such as patience, tolerance, and mutual understanding. Despite witnessing the harmful effects of

---

20. See this concept in Freire and Macedo, *Alfabetização*, 2011.

21. Concepts such as limit-situations, conscientization, and untested feasibility widely discussed in Freire's books will be discussed later.

capitalism, patriarchy, colonialism, racism, and other "isms," we still refuse to acknowledge their influence on our belief systems and seek justification for our flaws in the name of God. Regrettably, religions advocating for love, peace, and harmony in their discourses are often associated with intolerance and violence, mainly linked to politics, social, and economic inequalities. While many faithful individuals actively assist the poor and marginalized and promote reconciliation through their places of worship or international humanitarian organizations, much work still needs to be done to foster greater mutual regard and understanding beyond charitable events. Religious communities can and should be sites of hope and resistance. However, this will require stepping outside the comfort zone of like-minded religious organizations and engaging more deeply with international agencies and the public square to fight for justice in all fronts. Freire advocates for a problematizing education that challenges the traditional banking education model and points toward a collective vision that can create a more positive future by actively intervening and transforming our reality. Such a vision should be part of religious institutions that seek to promote the common good.

For the reasons mentioned above, it is imperative to create a planetary vision in which humans are part in order to inform, engage and support critical thinkers who can work to build a different kind of world—one that is not controlled by capitalism and its forms of production based on extractivism and devastation—but where all people and non-human species can coexist and thrive. Thus, the necessary educational approach capable of achieving these goals must involve principles that recognize human life as more important than means to economic ends, consider environmental and human costs, and contemplate people's well-being and the planet's long-term preservation.

Furthermore, it is crucial to encourage individuals to cultivate empathy for others and learn how interconnected everything is on the planet. This perspective needs to consider several aspects, including the impact of industrial growth and technological advancement on human lives and the planet, rather than just emphasizing economic gains. Religious and academic institutions should acknowledge their role as communities striving toward transformation through an educational process that avoids being a carbon copy of a dominant ideology. This approach will undoubtedly inspire all members to partake in a social movement toward justice and solidarity.

A Pedagogy for Planetary *Convivência*

The concept of planetary *convivência*—a term that I purposefully chose in place of the English word "conviviality"—will be developed later as I call attention to the educational process that can inform and foster coexistence between humans and more-than-humans. My argument is that most of our educational experiences did not adequately prepare us to understand how what happens locally affects people worldwide and the environment. Even though we know how everything is connected globally, we still lack the knowledge that, as ordinary people, we have the ability and responsibility to contribute to and participate in creating a safer, kinder, and more viable world. Globalization has made national borders more flexible to the flow of commodities and money, and certain peoples, while denying dignity to many who seek to flee violence and horrors caused by settler colonialism and American imperialism. However, this openness to international communication has also led to power struggles and new forms of colonialism, resulting in conflict and rivalry. Therefore, educating people for planetary *convivência* is a necessary work of our time that calls for a critical approach to tearing down and decolonizing the limiting conceptions of otherness.

This critical approach presupposes the development of an understanding of planetary belonging and recognizes the interdependence of other individuals for who they are and not for what they can provide or contribute. By recognizing that others do not threaten our safety or resources, we can strengthen our connections and appreciate the interdependence of our local and global environments. This mindset will allow us to continue to learn and grow. The challenge then shifts from "defining" pedagogy for planetary convivência, to figuring out "how to live it out." Pedagogy for planetary *convivência* must go beyond learning to meet, observe, and interact with others on a superficial level. It should be based on an ethic of care rooted in a planetary vision with ethical values that treat each human being and the creation as part of the same created order. It aims to highlight important aspects that will foster a pedagogical praxis,[22] enabling participants to enhance

---

22. The term praxis has in its essence the idea of critical reflection and transformative action. In his book *Pedagogy of the Oppressed*, Paulo Freire suggests that the term *praxis* implies critical reflection and transformation. His says: "people will be truly critical if they live the plenitude of the praxis, that is, if their action encompasses a critical reflection which increasingly organizes their thinking and thus leads them to move from a purely naïve knowledge of reality to a higher level." See Freire, *Pedagogy of the Oppressed*, 112. For a more thorough development of the Freirean concept of praxis, see Gadotti, *Pedagogy of Praxis,* ix–xvii.

their involvement in an ever-evolving world by acquiring the knowledge, skills, values, and attitudes necessary to thrive in their communities.

My proposal to achieve this goal is to embrace a praxis of planetary coexistence that incorporates compassion for people and the environment, along with critical thinking that denounces any and all unjust order. Throughout the upcoming chapters, I will delve into various ideas that are crucial for developing the foundation for a Pedagogy for Planetary *Convivência*. While these concepts may be presented separately for methodological purposes, they are ultimately interconnected and cannot be viewed in isolation. Although the list of topics covered is not exhaustive, you are encouraged, as a reader, to build upon and add to it. I hope the fundamental principles I have chosen to guide my approach toward a Pedagogy for Planetary *Convivência* will inspire you to initiate this critical dialogue.

Before delving into the specificities of the chapters, it is crucial to call attention to two words, *convivência* and pedagogy. The term *convivência* will be discussed throughout this book, but for now, it will do to know that it denotes the act of living together in each other's company. The term company, which derives from the Latin "*cum panis*" or the Iberian-Castilian "*con pañero*," refers to individuals with whom we share bread, people we are intimately connected to and dine with, or are seated at our table. Companions are those who share and endure the journey with us. This word is at the core of companionship, which signifies fellowship. As social creatures, we yearn for the presence of others, and when these interactions are healthy, they contribute to our overall well-being. The promotion of a positive learning environment is directly linked to the interactions and collaborative efforts of educators and learners, who both play important roles.

The concept of pedagogy has evolved throughout the years to take on certain traits to become what is currently referred to be a field of study that examines education in all its many and varied facets, involving more than just the technical aspects of education. It also encompasses promoting education in its cultural, philosophical, biological, psychological, historical, and social dimensions. As a discipline, pedagogy researches and analyzes all segments of educational phenomena. Unfortunately, there are occasions when an oversimplified and reductionist definition of pedagogy associates it just with procedures and techniques, trapping it in a scripted lesson format. Pedagogy is concerned with the sociopolitical and sociohistorical aspects of education, which serve as organizing principles for the methodological acts required to aid the educational process. According to

Henry Giroux,[23] pedagogy is a form of cultural production that includes creating and structuring knowledge, aspirations, values, and social practices that should advance the ideals of human dignity, liberty, and social justice. Thus, we can only strive toward a more just and equitable society if we know the social and political elements ingrained in our pedagogical practices. Freire's notion that pedagogy is a vision within which we strive to create a more humane world through education, that is, a vision beyond methods, is corroborated by Caribbean Jacqui Alexander who articulates this pedagogical concept saying,

> I came to understand pedagogies in multiple ways: as something given, as in handed, revealed; as in breaking through, transgressing, disrupting, displacing, inverting inherited concepts and practices, those psychic, analytic and organizational methodologies we deploy to know what we believe we know so as to make different conversations and solidarities possible; as both epistemic and ontological project bound to our beingness (. . .) pedagogies summons subordinated knowledge that are produced in the context of the practices of marginalization in order that we might destabilize existing practice of knowing and thus cross the fictive boundaries of exclusion and marginalization.[24]

Hence, pedagogy is not understood here in the instrumentalist sense of imparting knowledge or in relation to the educational system or schooled environments. Instead, pedagogy is seen as a praxis crucial to the social, political, ontological, and epistemic struggles of liberation; they are pedagogies of learning, unlearning, and learning again together, as Paulo Freire imagined.

---

23. Giroux, *Border Crossings*, 3–4.
24. Alexander, *Pedagogies of Crossing*, 7.

2

Buen Vivir towards a Planetary *Convivência*

> ¿Para qué sirve la utopía? Ella esta en el horizonte. Me acerco dos pasos y ella se aleja dos pasos. Camino diez pasos, y el horizonte se desplaza diez pasos más allá. A pesar de que camino, no la alcanzaré. ¿Para qué sirve la utopía? Sirve para esto: caminar.
>
> —Eduardo Galeano[1]

During the summer 2023, I had the opportunity to participate in the II International Conference on Environmental Education in the Amazon region in the city of Belém, state of Pará in Brazil. Among the different opportunities for exchange with the participants and speakers at the event, I had the opportunity to meet and chat briefly with a professor of that host University whose family was from the city I had recently visited. It was the beginning of a very beautiful exchange between us that provided the feeling of arriving at a land, territory, and family friendship with someone I didn't know. I felt we shared a connection because we had stepped on the

---

1. Galeano, *Las Palabras Andantes*, 230 (free translation: What is utopia for? She is on the horizon. I take two steps closer, and she takes two steps away. I walk ten steps, and the horizon advances by ten steps. Even if I walk, I won't catch up. What is the utopia for? For this: to walk).

same ground, breathed the same air, and had the same experiences: rivers, vegetation, and the local culture of our ancestors.

Following up on my conversation with the professor, I had the pleasure of meeting a descendant of the Kambeba indigenous people. We briefly introduced ourselves as she was going to speak next. She began with a song from her people, followed by poetry. When she started speaking, I was moved because what she shared was in tune with the topic I was going to discuss later. After her presentation, we had the opportunity to talk more. It was a sublime moment because with every word and smile exchanged, we felt a connection as deep as if we had known each other for a long time. There was mutual respect and admiration. It was a tender encounter where we recognized our experiences that, although lived in such different contexts, were part of our shared human history. Our relationship emerged in the sacred waters of solidarity and the narratives of our world as a shared space of memories, cultures, and aspirations.

This conference marked me deeply because it incorporated the meaning of what I seek to convey about coexistence, as there was a joint effort to change systems of domination through relationships, debates, and discussions about our scientific productions but, above all, about our pedagogical aspirations. I refer to these two encounters to illustrate how these experiences allowed us to recognize each other's gifts, passions, stories, struggles, and shared humanity. Whenever encounters like these happen, we are invited to expand our knowledge about ourselves and each other, as we seek better ways of living together. This is precisely what conviviality is: a form of social interaction that promotes friendship, a sense of belonging, and a gentle gesture toward the possibility of building communities together. These interactions teach us to value one another's gifts, even as we sometimes face potential conflicts. Even when cultures, identities, and experiences clash, we can still seek more just and respectful ways of relating to one another that dignify our existences. By strengthening our sense of community, shared responsibilities, and an awareness of our interdependence, we collaborate in building strong and healthy societies. In a globalized world driven by capitalism, individualism, and transactional relationships promoting conviviality can lose its impact and can become merely performative.

A case in point was a conference on Paulo Freire I attended in 2018 in another region of Brazil. At the opening of the Congress, we were welcomed by a "Congado" procession of indigenous students enrolled in the

Intercultural Formation for Indigenous Educators (FIEI) degree.[2] The students entered the space dancing, singing in their native languages, and greeting all participants. It was an incredibly moving opening event where we listened to the stories of struggles, resilience, and agency of the first inhabitants of Brazil who have been exercising survivance for hundreds of years, even in the face of brutality, extermination, and abandonment. Though we heard their stories, this academic setting was unable to create a space of *convivência* for its participants, and though the indigenous students had visibility during that specific part of the program, they were not part of the design of the conference, sharing in power and authority. They exposed their struggles, yet we did not build structures of accountability and action as conference participants. In other words, we did not build bonds grounded in the principles of *convivência*.

I highlight this episode because the path to conviviality is long, rocky, and full of obstacles. However, it is not impossible to embrace it if, as Eduardo Galeano reminds us, we are moved and inspired by utopia. Moving toward this utopia as members of an extended family, we discover that the difficulty in achieving it is not a flaw but a place to exercise our values and guiding principles further. The true worth lies not in reaching the utopia but in the pathway we forge as we continue moving toward it. Even knowing that the journey will be long and that we may be frightened by the dystopias along the way, we continue toward the target, conscious of the gift it is to walk together. All these elements strengthen us to resist perverse realities and all kinds of violence practiced against our fellow human beings and the planet.

This may imply the adoption, as Santos[3] suggests, of a "radical coexistence" where several epistemologies are recognized as equally valuable as the ancestral wisdom of the first inhabitants of the Americas. Sadly, many of our siblings have lost their linguistic connection to their ancestral culture, due to linguistic genocide—not to mention the extermination bodies, lands, cultures—where native languages have been exterminated. Eliminating a language is also a covert way to kill a people and its culture,

---

2. The Intercultural Formation for Indigenous Educators (FIEI) offered by the Faculty of Education (FaE) at the Federal University of Minas Gerais—UFMG was initially an extension course. Still, after the successful initial experience with indigenous teachers, it was offered in the context of the Support Program for Higher Education to the Indigenous Intercultural Degrees (PROLIND).

3. Sousa Santos, *Descolonizar el saber*, 2010.

in addition to constituting an astute way of immobilizing their actions and neutralizing their political power to articulate their ideas and desires.

Throughout this chapter, I examine the concept of conviviality and emphasize the importance of strengthening social bonds that value our irreducible dignity, even in the face of conflict and disagreements. Unfortunately, the current context of neoliberal and conservative policies does not promote conviviality, resulting in an increasing number of people experiencing insecurities of all kinds while being excluded from the economic system. Zygmunt Bauman noted that a democratic society's ability to succeed or fail rests on its ability to strike a balance between freedom and security.[4] For this reason, a liberation education must include the concept of *convivência*, which is founded on justice, dignity, and respect for both the environment and other people. This covers the goals and elements that are both theoretical and practical. In this book, I use the word *convivência* to highlight the implicit meaning that the Portuguese word carries, which is more about the subjective qualities and emotions people display when they share life together than it is about the actual physical experience of being together.

While coexistence is the translation to *convivência*, I believe it's important to distinguish one from another. As minoritized people can attest, folks can exist together without getting to know one another or being implicated in each other's wellbeing. For *convivência* to emerge, however, mutual flourishing is fundamental—there must be no place for invisibility, indifference, and disregard. On the contrary, the idea of *convivência* that I'm attempting to communicate suggests an orientation toward and a bond formed between individuals who regularly and closely interact with one another. This *convivência* proposes that individuals or communities must develop the ability to understand differences without feeling the need to fix them. The art of living together must allow inconsistencies, ambiguity, and discrepancies to exist alongside one another without being divisive or exclusionary. It cherishes human connections and focuses on the principles of collaboration and building reciprocal trust. As a fundamentally relational concept, *convivência* emphasizes the importance of being with others, and becoming with one another instead of striving to live a life based on individualism.

Exercising *convivência* can be challenging. Yet, it encourages a community to keep struggling through its dissonances to reach a common ground and common good that could enable members to come together and, through their differences and disparities, shape a community into being

---

4. Bauman, *Community*, 4–5.

that can exercise consent, collective becoming, and deal with disagreements so all can learn and expand the limits of their subjectivities collectively. *Convivência* requires intentional attitudes suffused with tolerance, respect, solidarity, and the ability to dialogue. That is, a space where people do not talk to, but with one another, always based on mutual respect. A space where communal experiences promote an environment that stimulates human flourishing—mentally, physically, and emotionally. There is no model or ideal space for *convivência*. Nevertheless, striving toward *convivência* is possible if we learn to encounter differences with a spirit of generosity and an open mind. As humans, we are wired for connections.

In today's fast-paced world, opting for *convivência*—that is, to enter into a place where all can be and become who they truly are, despite the dissonances that may unfold—can serve as a radical alternative to the ocean of disengagement, indifference, and competition that is drowning our relations to ourselves, one another, and the planet. As a result, *convivência* presents an inherent paradox of conflict and harmony, rigidity and fluidity, despair and hope.

While we may not be able to conceive of a perfect coexistence where cultural harmony and community cohesion thrive, we must not allow this to deter us from seeking *convivência* through the intentional disposition of minds and hearts. This effort, however, needs to be careful not to fall into the trap that tends to replace the ethnic other as a potentially dangerous subject who needs to be educated and "civilized," adapting to the norms established by a given community, usually a community in power. For these reasons, *convivência* requires diligent work to promote spaces where people can come together in all their multiplicity to develop deep bonds of affection, familiarity, and understanding. For many, convivial practices and the desire to embrace differences through affection and regard are deemed dangerous to a system that intentionally and insidiously produces subjectivities and desires based on profit, uniformity, alienation, and servility.

Historical Context of Conviviality

The concept of conviviality[5] has a long historical tradition and can be traced to the ancient Greeks and Romans. The word "convivial" comes

---

5. The Cambridge dictionary defines conviviality as relating to social events such as eating, drinking, and talking in friendly ways with others. Conviviality derives from the Latin *convīviālis* (festal), equivalent to the Latin *convīvi* (um) or feast and *convīv* (ere), to

from the Latin word "convivium," which means "to live together." In ancient times, conviviality was associated with feasting, drinking, and celebration. It served as a means of fostering community and commemorating life. In the Middle Ages, conviviality took on a more religious connotation. It was linked to the Spanish word "convivencia" to refer to a period in medieval Spain when Jews, Muslims, and Christians were able to live together on the Iberian Peninsula.

Between the 8th and 15th centuries, various cultural and religious groups thrived and built lively, vibrant, and diverse communities. This era was known as "convivencia," which was characterized by a culture of creative and intellectual accomplishments, as well as a dedication to respect and tolerance. Muslims, Christians, and Jews lived and worked together in the same neighborhoods, and individuals of different faiths frequently collaborated through the arts, literature, philosophy, architecture, and the sciences.[6]

One of the most famous examples of conviviality during the *Convivencia* period was the " School of Translators" in Toledo, where scholars from different faiths worked together to translate classical Greek and Arabic texts into Latin and Castilian. This collaboration led to a flourishing of intellectual and artistic achievement and helped to create a shared culture of learning, collaboration and innovation. Another example of conviviality during the *Convivencia* was the Alhambra Palace in Granada, which was built by Muslim and Jewish architects and artisans. The palace's design and decoration combined elements from both Islamic and Jewish artistic traditions, creating a unique and beautiful space that reflected the diversity and richness of these cultures.[7] Although not all experiences were "convivial" during this period, the members were able to create relevant artistic expressions by establishing adequate levels of interaction and tolerance. They integrated their views in various fields, including poetry, sculpture, architecture, science, law, and sacred texts, contributing to human history collectively.

The *Convivencia* period came to an end due to the Spanish Inquisition and the compulsory conversion or expulsion of Jews and Muslims.

---

live together and/or dine together.

6. Lovat and Crotty, *Reconciling Islam, Christianity and Judaism*, 103–18. See Mann et al., eds., *Convivencia: Jews, Muslims, and Christians in Medieval Spain*. This collection of essays examines how Jews, Muslims, and Christians interacted in the spheres of art and learning and how they influenced each other.

7. Irwin, *The Alhambra*. See also Brigitte Hintzen-Bohlen, *Andalusia: Art and Architecture*.

Religious extremism, regardless by whom it is practiced, has historically led to disastrous consequences, and remains a danger to humanity. Their radical actions exemplify the consequences of granting a dominant group elevated ethnic or racial status under the guise of religion.

In the modern era, conviviality has taken on a more political and social dimension, aiming to strengthen the possibilities of alliance amid differences. It suggests communicative strategies while sharing vulnerabilities by creating opportunities for social reparation and personal flourishing and producing resistance policies encompassing fluidity, solidarity, belonging, civic responsibility, and creative mutual support. It is from this frame of reference that I use the term *convivência*. This rich history of the term helps to interlace the threads for the meaning of *convivência*, which I seek to convey, particularly during this dark period of mass killing and genocidal tendencies we are living in.

Key Ideas on the Nature of Convivial Tool

Ivan Illich's *Tools for Conviviality* is an influential work in the field of social and political theory. Published in 1973, the book has had a lasting impact on debates around the nature of technology, education, and social organization. Illich was one of the first radical pedagogues who critically evaluated industrial society within an ecological framework, denouncing how technology could distort life's balance.[8] At its core, *Tools for Conviviality* is a critique of modern industrial society and its reliance on complex, centralized technologies that have created a world of passive consumers and disempowered individuals. Illich argues that a more convivial society, characterized by decentralized, simple, and accessible technologies, is not only possible but necessary for human flourishing.

Illich criticizes modern industrial society, stating that the primary approach to technological development is flawed. According to him, people rely on technology for even their basic daily needs due to industrial development. And, to maintain interdependence and dignity while avoiding being overwhelmed by machines, individuals must choose encounters and spaces that promote conviviality.[9] Because convivial spaces enhance

---

8. Ivan Illich, Austrian Roman Catholic priest, theologian, philosopher, and social critic, founder of the progressive Centro Intercultural de Documentación (Intercultural Center for Documentation) in Cuernavaca, Mexico.

9. Illich, *Tools for Conviviality*, 11.

interpersonal interactions, support autonomy and agency, and offer an option out of technocratic catastrophe, Illich suggests that all members of a society must "learn to reverse the present deep structure of tools" in a society dominated by machines, and instead create places for encounter that guarantee their rights.[10]

Illich's ideas challenged his 1970s audience to reconsider the paradigm of technological development and its implications. As an acute observer of the industrialization process and the advancement of capitalism of that time, Illich was concerned that not all members of society would have the same opportunities to enjoy life in the company of one another. He attempted to restore the primacy of "being" over "having" by exposing the flaws in technology and capitalism and encouraging people to identify when technologies become manipulative and life-threatening. His critique of modern industrial society also significantly impacted how education and learning were perceived then and now. He contended that modern educational systems were overly focused on producing passive information consumers rather than empowering people to seek to learn autonomously and through experience of conviviality.

Convivialist Manifesto

At a colloquium in Tokyo in 2010, the topic of conviviality and convivialism was discussed. The colloquium heavily emphasized the works of Ivan Illich, drawing new perspectives from his insights. In 2011, the contributions made to the colloquium by Alain Caillé, Marc Humbert, Serge Latouche, and Patrick Viveret were published under the title *De la convivialité: Dialogues sur la société conviviale à venir*.[11]

Later, in 2014, a group of academics from various disciplines, including philosophy, sociology, political science, and economics, published *The Convivialist Manifesto*. The document stresses the necessity of developing international cooperation systems based on novel social structures and novel perspectives on nature in response to ecological depletion. Additionally, it lists numerous coexistence-based projects that have already been put into practice on a variety of fronts.[12] The authors characterize this group

---

10. Illich, *Tools for Conviviality*, 10.

11. *Convivialist Manifesto: A Declaration of Interdependence. Global Dialogues* 3 (2014) 7. M. Clarke, trans. https://doi.org/10.14282/2198–403-GD-3.

12. *Convivialist Manifesto*, 24.

endeavor as a search for a coexistence where all efforts are focused on the common welfare. The authors contend that convivialism is not a novel doctrine but rather a process of mutual questioning that cannot be reduced to a singular approach to solving humanity's issues in light of the fact that natural resources are finite. Moreover, convivialism is a way of being together that seeks to protect what each person understands as most valuable to ensure all attitudes of cooperation, communication, and nonviolence.

The main point of the Manifesto is that contemporary societies are characterized by a hyper-individualistic and consumerist culture that promotes selfishness, materialism, and competition. These traits are dangerous because they can lead to problems with social cohesion, ecological sustainability, and human flourishing. The economic paradigm of neoliberalism, which prioritizes individual liberty, market efficiency, and profit maximization over social justice, well-being, and ecological sustainability, reflects this culture. This culture causes social fragmentation and has adverse effects on both society and the environment.

In addition, excessive consumption and pollution caused by consumerism and the pursuit of economic growth have resulted in environmental destruction and climate change. The Manifesto highlights the limitations of the individualist and consumerist model of growth and warns of the dangers it poses to both human societies and the planet. For instance, climate change is a threat to life, livelihoods, and all creation around the world. It increases poverty and inequality and harms the ability of communities, particularly indigenous and poor people, to live full, dignified lives. Therefore, they propose a society that values collaboration, solidarity, and environmental awareness. The Manifesto provides recommendations on how to achieve this, such as promoting sustainable growth, involving citizens in decision-making, and protecting species and ecosystems.

The document strongly emphasizes how interdependent people and nature are and acknowledges the finite nature of natural resources. It proposes a circular economy, which reduces pollution while reusing and recycling resources. Additionally, it proposes a holistic strategy for education that incorporates social, environmental, and economic factors. In short, the Manifesto advocates for a new societal paradigm that fosters conviviality, or a sense of shared well-being and cooperation. Thus, it emphasizes the importance of education to cultivate respect for the environment, to recognize the limits of natural resources, and to prioritize the common good over individual interests.[13]

In 2020, the Second Convivialist Manifesto was published as a follow-up to the first one. It expands upon the original ideas and addresses the challenges of a post-neoliberal society. The Manifesto argues that neoliberalism, which has been the primary economic model for the past forty years, has not fulfilled its commitments to promote economic growth, social equity, and individual autonomy. Instead, it has led to disparities in society, environmental destruction, and a decline in democratic values.[14]

The second document's focus on the value of localism is one of its most significant additions. It argues that the loss of variety and homogenization of culture are the results of the globalized economic system. To counteract this, the Manifesto advocates for localism, prioritizing local economies and communities to promote convivialism. It emphasizes the need to address societal problems at their core rather than just treating their symptoms. The Manifesto asserts that contemporary social problems, such as social and economic inequality, are not natural or unavoidable, but rather the outcomes of specific historical and political processes. To address these underlying causes, it is necessary to reevaluate societal values and commit to systemic change. Another inclusion is the understanding of the value of nurturing and care in promoting conviviality. The Manifesto makes the case that although care is frequently undervalued and disregarded in modern societies, it is crucial for developing bonds of unity and support. The Manifesto suggests that care should be a fundamental value in a convivialist society.[15] The Second Convivialist Manifesto offers a convincing proposal based on the principles of conviviality, social equity, and environmental preservation. It outlines a roadmap for a fairer, more sustainable future by suggesting reforms to redefine the government's role, encourage communal and ecological resources, promote economic diversity and decolonization, and strengthen democratic governance. Conviviality, according to the Manifesto, "is not an idealistic fantasy but a real possibility that can be realized through collective action and political mobilization."[16]

---

13. *Convivialist Manifesto. A Declaration of Interdependence* (Global Dialogues 3). Duisburg 2014: Käte Hamburger Kolleg / Centre for Global Cooperation Research (KHK / GCR21), 2014, 21–37.

14. "The Second Convivialist Manifesto: Towards a Post-Neoliberal World." *Civic Sociology* (2020) 1–24.

15. "The Second Convivialist Manifesto."

16. Manifesto, 17.

Both Manifestos suggest a new approach to societal values and objectives that prioritize cooperation, environmental awareness, and conviviality. The first Manifesto laid the groundwork for these concepts, while the second expanded and deepened the discussion. Both provide a valuable critique of modern cultures, encouraging us to re-examine our beliefs and actions while striving for a more just, cordial, and viable world. The authors suggest a new ethical standard based on reciprocity, solidarity, and care, drawing from diverse sources. They offer guidance on how to tackle contemporary social and ecological issues by promoting a new political, economic, and cultural paradigm. The challenge now is to turn this vision into reality.

Despite the significance of these documents in current debates, they do not sufficiently consider diverse epistemic viewpoints and their potential to promote conviviality. Therefore, addressing epistemic injustice, or what Santos defines as epistemicide,[17] and cognitive extractivism,[18] as named by renowned Michi Saagiig Nishnaabeg scholar, Leanne Betasamosake Simpson, will substantially advance the nuances of conviviality. Cognitive extractivism refers to the assimilation of technologies or ideas from indigenous cultures without proper credit to their creators by the dominant culture. For this reason, it is crucial to consider forms of knowledge and wisdom generated in resistance against abyssal exclusion and political nullification so that new horizons are opened regarding the world's cultural, political, and epistemic diversity.[19] Santos believes that cognitive justice can be achieved by utilizing both the ecology of knowledges and intercultural translation. According to him, the ecologies of knowledges are collective cognitive constructions guided by the principles of horizontality and reciprocity. This implies that the differences between various ecologies are acknowledged non-hierarchically and strengthened by the development of complementary relationships between them.[20] Thus, to encourage and welcome alternative epistemologies, we must understand them in a spirit of solidarity and reciprocity.

---

17. Sousa Santos, *Epistemologies of the Global South*, 2014.
18. Sousa Santos and Meneses, *Knowledges Born in the Struggle*, 207.
19. Sousa Santos and Meneses, *Knowledges Born in the Struggle*, xv.
20. Sousa Santos and Meneses, *Knowledges Born in the Struggle*, xx.

A Pedagogy for Planetary *Convivência*

From *Con-Vivere* to *Bene-Vivere*

When taken literally, the Latin word "con-vivere" alludes to the act of living with. It implies that community members can live in harmony with one another and, ideally, communicate in a respectful and friendly manner. However, human connections are not always easy and harmonious, and, as painful as it is to admit, disagreements and conflicts are common in human interactions. On rare occasions, these conflicts can contribute to broadening the narrow perspective of some when confronted with more expansive perspectives. The tension between the need for human beings to be together and the conflicts that sometimes arise in this being together is creatively expressed by Leonardo Boff in his book *O Despertar da Águia* (*The Awakening of the Eagle*).[21] Boff highlights this tension by introducing the definitions of two words—the symbolic and the diabolical—that coexist dialectically in human interactions.

Boff explains that the term "symbol" has its roots in the ancient Greek word *symbállein*, or *symbállesthai*. This word means to throw something so that it sticks together. It alludes to various realities that are united from various points, or to various forces that converge in a single direction. In contrast, the word "diabolical" is derived from the Greek word *dia-ballein*, meaning to cast something away randomly and aimlessly. Unlike the symbolic, the diabolic disengages, segregates, separates, and opposes. The two aspects of human existence often clash and intertwine, whether in personal or societal contexts. Sometimes pleasant attitudes can be seen in the joyous gatherings, acts of unity, and celebrations of love and friendship. However, there are also moments when hate, division, discord, and severance prevail in human interactions. It's reasonable to assume that the realities of *symbállein* and *diaballein* interact dynamically and never truly vanish. As a result, they are constantly in flux, striving to reach a balance between these opposing forces.

The natural world has demonstrated that explosions and mutations can create cosmic order and organization. In nature, one can observe patterns of competition, survival, independence, and complementarity. However, this dialectical relationship poses an ethical challenge for humans, who must strive for peaceful coexistence with each other and the ecosystem that supports them. The overuse of natural resources and the increase in ethnic and religious conflicts have put life on the planet in great danger.

21. Boff, *O Despertar da Águia*, 11–13.

Buen Vivir towards a Planetary *Convivência*

As intelligent and creative beings, we can work together and preserve our human sensitivities finding new ways of living in harmony. Rather than creating divisions, we can bring ourselves closer to each other and to our planet by thinking critically about our world and our interactions. We can cultivate empathy and compassion and listen to the wisdom passed down from our ancestors. By paying attention to our hearts and our bodies, we can take actions that promote unity and respect for our environment.

The Ancestral Understanding of *Convivência*

In an agonizing world facing multifaceted economic, ecological, political, and civilizational crises, we need to learn from those who live together as a community and in harmony with nature, never losing their connection to the earth. They are the guardians of some of the world's remaining forests and biodiversity hotspots. Even in the face of invasion and oppression perpetrated against their people and way of life, they often have remained firm in their purposes. Indigenous peoples' ancient worldview challenges the notion that they are barbaric and lack wisdom. They possess invaluable knowledge closely intertwined with nature and all that exists on Earth. While we may aspire to possess their wisdom, it is not easy to replicate their way of life. The lifestyles of such individuals exist outside of the globalized culture and cannot be easily commodified for mass consumption. Those who seek power and monetary gain hold contrasting views compared to those who prioritize the interconnectedness of life and value interdependent relationships over individual rights. The latter group has a perspective that encompasses the "cosmic significance of life" and displays unconditional respect for both human and non-human life.

The concept of *convivência*, as understood by our ancestors, aims to emphasize vital aspects of the life and worldview of the initial inhabitants of Latin America. This is intended to expand our understanding of *convivência*, inspired by the Guarani culture. For instance, the Guarani language spoken by many indigenous groups from different regions of South America includes an expression—*Teko Porã*—that brings an expansive meaning to the word *convivência*.[22] In Guarani, words like *Teko*, which translates as

---

22. The Guarani indigenous people are located in five South American countries: Argentina, Brazil, Bolivia, Paraguay, and Uruguay. According to the Brazilian Institute of Geography and Statistics (IBGE), based on the 2010 Census, there are 305 ethnic groups in Brazil and at least 274 languages. Although the Guarani from these countries share

"existing in a community," and *Porã*, which means "beautiful or good," are employed to describe a way of being that is in tune with nature. The Pachamama, or Mother Earth, is revered and protected by the Guarani people, who consider nature and humans to be one and the same. The diversity of species in the world comprises both human and non-human species. *Teko* embodies the Guarani people's long-standing yearning for harmony with all creation. According to Guarani culture, the land cannot be owned as it is seen as a living ecosystem, home to many other living beings. In Guarani culture, to be recognized as a person one must be understood as someone integrated into the natural environment. For them, the planet is more than just a place; it is a cherished home to countless other living beings. Kristina Takuá, an indigenous educator, offers a summary saying:

> Teko Porã, as a philosophical, political, social and spiritual concept that expresses exactly this great Web, where we live in balance, respect and harmony; is the representation of the good way of being and living . . . For the Guarani people, there is no tekó without Tekoá; that is, there is no way of being without the place of being. So, you must have land, with forest, with water and with all your life included to be able to live your culture and to be Guarani. Experiencing the full meaning of Good Living these days can often seem contradictory, due to various situations that move us away from it, and lead us to the "Tekó Vai", the Evil Living.[23]

Teko is a philosophy that emphasizes the importance of valuing both our environment and the people we encounter. Therefore, no matter what justifications we use—whether ideological, ethnic, gender, or religious—acts of violence only serve to diminish our humanity. Anything that disrupts the delicate balance of the universe, endangers the environment, or harms others, falls into this category.

---

commonalities, they also have slight differences regarding languages and cosmovision. The meaning of this concept, *Teko*, is shared among most of them even when they use a different word to express. The Guarani language belongs to the Tupi-Guarani linguistic trunk, from which 21 languages are derived. It is the most widely spoken indigenous language in South America and reaches 60% of Paraguay. In Mato Grosso, Brazil, border schools teach it at the school. A considerable number of words used in the Brazilian vocabulary come from Tupi-Guarani language.

23. Takuá. *Rebento*, 5–8. Cristine Takuá is an indigenous teacher. Graduated in Philosophy from UNESP—Marília, teaches classes in Philosophy, Sociology, History and Geography in EE Txeru Ba'e Kua-I, DER Santos, belonging to the Indigenous Land Ribeirão Silveira, located on the border of the municipalities of Bertioga and São Sebastião. She is one of the acting leaders of the Guarani Yvyrupa Commission.

Buen Vivir towards a Planetary Convivência

The Quéchua expression *Sumak Kawsay* and the Ayamara *Suma Qamaña* both have the same meaning as the Guarani *Teko Porã*. All these expressions concern *buen vivir*, which translates roughly into English as "living well." It is a cosmovision that supports and gives meaning to the social structure of South America's first inhabitants. It is characterized as a life of goodness and beauty, rooted in community and harmony with other people and nature. As Blanca Chancoso, Ecuadorian educator and indigenous leader of the Otavalo people, beautifully describes,

> Sumak Kawsay, in literal translation, would be life in fullness, excellence, the best, the beautiful. But, interpreted in political terms, it is life itself, a mixture of actions and political wills that mean changes so that the people do not lack their daily bread so that these social inequalities between men and women do not exist. Sumak Kawsay is the dream not only of indigenous peoples but also of all humans.[24]

The concept of *buen vivir*, which values collective well-being and harmony with nature over individual success, is a common belief among indigenous cultures worldwide, and is not just limited to the Andean or Amazonian regions. This perspective on life is shared by the original inhabitants of Latin America, who prioritize reciprocal thriving rather than striving to outdo others. Such a vision of well-being, as fundamentally collective as survival, depends on various forms of codependency, including our codependency with nature, which we often irresponsibly devastate.

Paulo Suess, theological advisor to the CIMI (Indigenous Missionary Council),[25] claims that this cosmovision, conveyed in the expression *Sumak Kawsay*, is comprised of memory and horizon. The restoration of a horizon—a future with justice and equality—the creation of new utopias, and the strengthening of ancestors' knowledge are more important than its immediate execution of a break with everything that threatens life.

The indigenous struggle for *buen vivir* is part of a larger alliance seeking to safeguard the world we inhabit. It's not a fixed set of rules, a prescription to follow, but rather a way of thinking and living. It is a worldview to embrace. To adopt this perspective and strive towards it, one must be drawn to this way of being and existing in the world. Within this cosmovision, the

---

24. Acosta, *O Bem Viver- Uma Oportunidade para Imaginar outros mundos*, 11 (free translation by the author).

25. Bonin, *Encarte Pedagógico* X (2016) 2. Available: https://www.cimi.org.br/pub/Porantim/2015/Encarte_Porantim381_dez2016.pdf

past is respected and honored. It is considered as a time that sustains the continuous production of the present and points to the future, inspired by the ancestral reservoir of wisdom.[26]

As a result, the past is interpreted as an immersion in *buen vivir*, a harmonious *convivência* between people and nature where reciprocity-based values co-inspire respect, fraternal friendship, and a deep appreciation of all species on Earth. According to this way of thinking, living is a process that results in our *buen vivir*. As Egon Heck and Francisco Loebens say,

> Indigenous peoples arrive at the beginning of the 21st century not just as survivors, but as peoples with rich cultures and ancient wisdom. It is from this place that we consider them important social, political, and ethnic actors, making important contributions to the construction of new life projects in different countries.[27]

Indigenous cultures place great importance on spirituality, primarily expressed through songs, dances, rituals for special occasions, and prayers. For instance, the Guarani stopped farming their land after the missionaries forbade them from celebrating their festivals in the sixteenth century. Their way of life demonstrates that they produce and work to survive rather than living to produce. Understanding that our power derives from our respectful relationship to the land physically and spiritually is a crucial lesson we can learn from indigenous peoples' way of existence and their profound connection to all humans and more-than-humans. Indigenous peoples draw inspiration from their connection to the land and the cosmos for their physical vigor and spiritual power. Life and sustenance depend on planting and harvesting, which should always be done with reverence for Mother Earth. This cosmovision challenges us to problematize the Western idea of progress, emphasizing the need for respect towards the Earth, which is vital for humanity's survival. Ritual songs and dances that convey joy and appreciation are essential for restoring the strength to overcome difficulties. Indigenous people have a deep reverence for nature and use resources efficiently. Their way of life, *buen vivir*, involves a reciprocal relationship between planting, harvesting, and giving thanks through dances and rituals. When prevented from participating in these ceremonies, life is incomplete.

---

26. Suess. *Elementos para a busca do Bem Viver*. https://cimi.org.br/2010/12/elementos-para-a-busca-do-bem-viver-sumak-kawsay-para-todos-e-sempre/

27. Bonin, *Encarte Pedagógico* X (2016) 4. Available: https://www.cimi.org.br/pub/Porantim/2015/Encarte_Porantim381_dez2016.pdf.

Buen Vivir towards a Planetary *Convivência*

In Ecuador and Bolivia, indigenous worldviews, which prioritize harmony with nature over economic development, are now protected by law. When Rafael Correa was elected president in 2007 with the support of indigenous groups, his government helped create a new constitution that embraced the concept of *buen vivir*, making Ecuador the first country to grant constitutional rights to nature. The Correa administration had unveiled the National Plan for Good Living spanning from 2009 to 2013, outlining a long-term strategy to steer Ecuador's public policies and activities toward *buen vivir*. Unfortunately, these initial undertakings and promises to transform Ecuador's economy fundamentally did not result in any significant changes. The development of enormous copper deposits threatens culturally and environmentally significant portions of the Ecuadorian Amazon, which runs counter to the ideals of *buen vivir*. Extractivist activities that prioritize profit-making and the exploitation of natural resources go against the indigenous worldview. They promote a utilitarian model that benefits the wealthy while disregarding the needs of the poor. These actions are driven by an insatiable desire to acquire land, natural resources, and labor through colonial means.

Thus, the neoliberal scheme constitutes a pernicious system that requires us to have a critical conscience to combat its tricks because they are hidden in many ways, behind expensive pharmaceuticals, synthetic dietary supplements, high-performance physical activities, and even meditation techniques, which, in essence, are nothing more than strategies to encourage consumption and attract more consumers. According to neoliberal rationality, such strategies function as mechanisms to regulate subjectivities and homogenize desires. Without realizing it, we have become puppets of the "invisible hand of the market'" (Adam Smith, 1759). Additionally, any self-centered approach, whether in the educational or religious spheres, must be rigorously examined because it runs against the essential principles of *buen vivir*, which emphasize the simplicity of communal living and the interdependence of all created beings.

The ethos of individualism is antisocial, as it disregards the human being as a social being who, as mentioned previously, needs connectivity with others and with nature to achieve a balanced form of *buen vivir*. Therefore, we might envision human life from the multiple perspectives of connectivity, balance, and inclusion by dialectically identifying the distinctions between symbolic and demonic forces. As Boff says, "[n]obody just exists. All inter-exist and coexist." Therefore, considering an unpredictable global situation, it is our responsibility to look for lifestyle alternatives that will allow us to maintain both the planet's life and our own, especially the lives of the most vulnerable. It is crucial to consider new types of coexisting to preserve the humanizing quality of our existence. To accomplish our vision of unity in diversity, the objective is to re-establish the connection between people and nature while re-evaluating the many dimensions of our communal existence.

It's possible that we don't have to venture too far to realize the importance of building positive relationships with others, valuing our unique qualities, and being receptive to the goodness within us to extend that to others. It is important for us to be aware of our daily interactions and recognize these qualities within ourselves and our own group. Although it may be easier to observe the shortcomings of others, such as their differences, prejudices, flaws, and lack of respect, we should take the time to reflect on our own actions. Sometimes it's easy to label those who believe differently than we as intolerant when it comes to religion. However, we often forget that we may also be contributing to a negative atmosphere of hostility and disinterest, whether knowingly or unknowingly.

As individuals who follow a particular faith, we may sometimes fail to recognize our lack of tolerance towards others or are unable to see the violent tendencies that our religious practices may create. More specifically for Christians, it is crucial to remember how Jesus was always deeply moved by the pain and struggles of those often marginalized by society. He never prioritized social status, gender, or nationality over the inherent value and dignity of each human being. Christians, however, may sometimes deviate from Jesus' teachings when their palliative charitable actions do not address the root causes of social injustices. Such actions often, hidden in their unbridled greed, attempt to assuage the guilt of their addiction to material accumulation that, invariably, denies others their share of the earth's bounty.

Jesus lived and preached during a time of profound injustice, where the ruling power and its allies demanded the sacrifice of a significant portion of the population to maintain their control. Although this era is now in the distant past, it bears resemblance to today, where resources are distributed unevenly. For instance, during the COVID-19 pandemic, billionaires doubled their fortunes while millions of workers around the world experienced stagnation in their living standards. While billionaires celebrated an incredible increase in their fortunes, the pandemic derailed decades of progress in combating extreme poverty, increasing its toll.

In his time, Jesus was an inspiring figure who welcomed those marginalized by a society that inflicted suffering, injustice, and exclusion on its members. With a compassionate heart, Jesus consistently demonstrated integrity and compassion, overcoming cultural prejudices, religious legalism, and the oppressive power of the Roman Empire. He spoke empathetically to vulnerable individuals and inspired his followers to creatively resist and break cycles of violence, thus restoring hope for a transformed world. In the gospel narrative, according to Luke, Jesus takes on Isaiah's prophecy: "The Spirit of the Lord is upon me, because he has anointed me to preach the gospel to the poor; He has sent me to proclaim release to captives and recovery of sight to the blind, to let the oppressed go free, and to proclaim the year of the Lord's favor" (Luke 4:18–19). Thus, in his ministry, Jesus defends the oppressed, following the tradition of the Old Testament prophets. He presents a new way of living and interacting with others. His example motivates us to adopt similar ways of behavior that reflect his genuine spirit of *convivência*.

As individuals who follow a spiritual path and strive for a conscious existence, it is vital that we recognize the importance of promoting peaceful *convivência* on our planet. We should strive to establish cooperative and democratic connections by nurturing care and respect for both humans and the environment. However, in a world where affectionate relationships are rare, it's not adequate to just witness instances of amicable coexistence among individuals. We must intentionally educate ourselves and others on how to coexist respectfully. This task requires the participation of everyone. Remaining open to learning and observing, as well as practicing attentive listening, allows us to hear the sounds of nature, observe the natural world, and understand its teachings. We must be mindful of the unspoken words of those disregarded in our societies and gain a deeper understanding of our internal and external realities. Doing so allows us to engage in new channels beyond our rational and analytical thinking. Merely reading books, researching climate change, disapproving of religious intolerance, or denouncing the deterioration of human relationships based on self-interest will not enable us to advance *convivência*. It is essential to take a deliberate approach to acknowledging the significance of both our external and internal worlds, where life flourishes and progresses. To bring about a civilizing transformation that recognizes nature as a subject of rights, we must overcome the separation of humans from nature and the anthropocentric, patriarchal, and colonial designs that cause planetary destruction.

A new pact of social and environmental coexistence is required to promote harmony. This involves learning to read the world critically and recognizing the promises and limitations of every circumstance. It is also crucial to restore and reaffirm values that can promote the defragmentation of interpersonal relationships, allowing for a new planetary consciousness. This mission belongs to all citizens, but religious individuals, given what they preach and seemingly believe, are responsible for sharing a vision of harmony, peace, love, and compassion, which are core values in major religions, in order to prevent exclusivist views that promote hatred and violence as we are, sadly, witnessing in all corners of the world.

When we neglect to connect with our inner selves, others, and nature, we miss out on the intricate threads that make up the web of life and give meaning to our existence. It's important to remember that we are both tiny beings in the vast universe but also spiritual beings with a spark of divinity. As active participants and co-creators of our lives, it's our responsibility to learn from nature and our ancestors and embrace the interconnectedness of all things as a blessing from our Creator. *Teko* reminds us that the Guarani people's millennial experience is centered around the pursuit of harmony between nature and humans. This harmony is maintained through the reciprocal relationships between all created things and is a crucial feature of a dignified material and social existence. It is essential to prioritize these connections over any form of prejudice, whether it is based on race, culture, religion, or any other ranking of importance.

We can all learn from the ancestral wisdom of indigenous peoples, which translates into respect for life, the environment, creatures big and small, mountains and rivers. I believe that by adopting these values, it will be possible to build a world where it is easier to love, as Paulo Freire said, a world where poetry, art, philosophy, literature, politics, science, technology, and our spirituality are intrinsically intertwined, helping us to promote an affectionate planetary *convivência*. Embracing an epistemic rupture that rejects a linear, individualistic logic and unjust social systems is absolutely necessary for a more circular, diverse vista and fresh hope to emerge. Just like the concept of Ubuntu,[28] Teko is in direct contrast to the concept of "I" in Western society.

---

28. The African concept of *ubuntu* (Shona, Ndebele, or Zulu) stands in contrast, ontologically and epistemologically, to the western worldview in which a person is defined

Buen Vivir towards a Planetary Convivência

The African expression, *Umntu ngumtu ngabantu*, which translates as "a person is a person through other persons" in the African ethos, emphasizes that being is always being in relation to and with others.[29] As Martin Luther King Jr. said beautifully, "we are caught in an inescapable web of mutuality, tied together in a single garment of fate. What affects one directly affects all indirectly."[30] We are trustworthy members of a fragile web of connections, belonging to a delicate network of relationships, with intrinsic value not measured by external attributes, but by heart and character. Each of us is precious in the eyes of the Creator, regardless of race, education, gender, ethnicity, social, or economic status. We all need to be taken care of and deserve respect. Therefore, everything that threatens or undercuts the interdependence and common harmony between people and the rest of creation must be disregarded. As human beings, we need each other, and we all need the natural resources that make human life on Earth possible. Thus, from the feeling of union and belonging comes the responsibility to care for others, for the community, for Mother Earth, at the same time that we are cared for by others. This image of an interdependent world cannot be embraced by an egocentric, individualistic, and narcissistic worldview that fosters a culture of hostility, violence, and otherness that results in conflicts, economic instability, environmental catastrophes, and strained relationships.

Unless we learn with others that we belong together, we will not overcome the insularity in which we are immersed. We must therefore educate ourselves on how to interact, connect, and coexist. To recover this sense of being with the other as part of who we are, we must go through a conversion process, a *metanoia*, through which we embrace new ways of being. This is not an easy process to undertake because many factors try to restrict and conform us to ways of being contrary to our human vocation *to be more* in a Freirean sense. What makes us human is precisely this assumption that in our finitude we are in a permanent movement of search. Freire's insights resemble the thoughts of Tutu and MLK when in *Pedagogy of Freedom* he says,

> For this reason, women and men by mere fact of being *in* the world are also necessarily being *with* world. Our being is a being *with*. So, to be in the world without making history, without being made

---

by the unconstrained "I" in relation to the self and its inner being, its self-determination, rather than by its sense of dependence and relation to others. See Hampson and Whalen, *Tales of the Heart*.

29. Tutu, *God Is Not a Christian*, 21.
30. M. L. King, *Why We Can't Wait*, 65.

A Pedagogy for Planetary *Convivência*

by it, without creating culture, without a sensibility toward one's own presence in the world, without a dream, without song, music, or painting, without caring for the earth or the water, without using one's hand, without sculpturing or philosophizing, without any opinion about the world, without doing science or theology, without awe in the face of mystery, without learning, instruction, teaching, without ideas on education without being political, is a total impossibility.[31]

Convivência, therefore, is the cultivation of the human potential for kindness, compassion, care, and openness. It demands that we consider the needs of a depleted planet as well as the physical, emotional, mental, and spiritual necessities of individuals. It encourages us to acknowledge and identify the difficulties we encounter every day in life as well as the constraints and potentially destructive emotions we may experience within ourselves. *Convivência* is the ongoing process of honing our *consciousness of* and *capacity for* welcoming the other's presence. It entails improving our capacity to acknowledge our flaws and restrictions, as well as our positive traits. In our mutual fallibility lies, potentially, ways to be better, to be attentive, and to be generous with others and with ourselves.

When extending a greeting, people in some nations bow toward one another while placing their palms over their chests: "I bowed to the divine presence within you," is what this gesture conveys. This mutual acknowledgment affirms the other's integrity by highlighting the fact that we are all formed of the same substances and the Creator breathed God's own life into each of us. Even though we all have unique qualities, dispositions, and outward traits, we share the essential characteristics of being human. As we rely on each other and are part of a larger whole, it's crucial to cultivate kindness and respect in our daily interactions. This strengthens the bond between the environment, other people, and us. To learn how to get along with each other, we must abandon the capitalist-imposed patterns of unchecked individualism that mostly cause division, prejudice, and hurt. If we want to unlearn them, we must reject methods of knowing that overlook these connections. We must also unlearn the habits that promote egotism, individualism, and competition, characteristics that are intrinsic to capitalist ways of being in the world.

To truly understand *convivência* on a planetary level, we must let go of the idea that we can handle difficult situations on our own. *Convivência*

---

31. Freire, *Pedagogy of Freedom,* 57–58.

is about working together, with a spirit of reciprocity and cooperation, to create a shared vision. If we want to establish a new paradigm of planetary *convivência*, we must view our environment, community, country, and interactions with others as integral parts of ourselves. This means having a deep love and compassion for the entire planet and all its inhabitants, human and more-than-humans.

3

Social Responsibility for Planetary *Convivência*

> History as a time of possibility presupposes human beings' capacity for observing, discovering, comparing, evaluating, deciding, breaking away, and for being responsible. It implies their ability to be ethical, as well as their capacity for ethical transgression. It is not possible to educate for democracy, for freedom, for ethical responsibility with a deterministic understanding of history.
>
> —Paulo Freire[1]

IN MANY PARTS OF the world, democracy is currently fragile and unstable due to the reemergence of nationalism, fundamentalism, and extremist political and religious views. In recent decades, religious and non-religious groups have risen in the public space in different parts of the globe with actions that can be classified as "fundamentalist." Although these radical narratives express themselves in different dimensions of culture, the religious aspect occupies a prominent place because fundamentalist groups find in religion the necessary support to promote and perpetuate an exclusionary worldview validated by a punitive and vengeful God. In general terms,

---

1. Freire, *Pedagogy of Indignation*, 113.

fundamentalism categorizes positions of authoritarianism, intolerance, intransigence, fanaticism, denial of plurality, and refusal of dialogue. People who use such actions have a reactionary view of social changes and use such "fundamentals" to persuade society to fight against "enemies."

Although religious fundamentalism is not exclusive to one religion, in the current state of affairs, we might think that, from a Christian perspective, it has played a vital role in making politics a detestable holy war of "good" versus "evil," leading to a series of dynamics of hatred and polarization between the different social segments of society. For instance, as Virginia Garrard argues, Pentecostals in Latin America have generally tended to define their moral principles in terms of "the church" and "the world." Historically, they have believed that the world outside of the church is demonic and deadly, and that Christians should only interact with it through prayer and evangelizing efforts. According to her,

> As evangelical religion becomes more established in Latin America, an increasing number of evangelical, mainly Pentecostal/Neopentecostal, churches have adopted the hermeneutics of political engagement derived from a movement known as "Christian Restoration," the international derivation of which is known as "Dominion theology."[2]

The author defines "dominion theology" as a subset of political evangelism that seeks to elevate a group of conservative Christians to positions of political authority in order to establish "dominion" over the planet and expedite the coming of God's Kingdom. Moreover, according to Garrard, dominion theology "is not so much a 'theology' per se so much as it is an ideology and practice for a specific type of conservative Christian political engagement derived from Christian Restorationism."[3]

For fundamentalists in general, and more specifically neo-Pentecostals, narratives and actions convert into a new form of fascism as they violently combat those who do not adapt to their vision and principles. Among the many strategies used to undermine the foundations of the fragile democracy, hate speeches disguised in a nationalist, pro-life, pro-family narratives, and the dissemination of conspiracy theories, have been used to manipulate the religious imagination of the people by attracting them into a messianic dimension through which people naively portrayed themselves as saviors of a new order. As Garrard indicates,

2. Garrard, *Religions*, 2.
3. Garrard, *Religious*, 4.

> This is precisely the milieu in which secular political ambition and religious principles can readily meld with one another to create a single ideology supported by a powerful moral panic that feeds off code words, unquestioning obedience, and a faith-vindicated fear of the Other. This is hegemony by consent in the most Gramscian sense: in return for submitting to a closed-circuit of authority and self-referential verities, followers believe they are following God's will and will thus receive God's favor and eternal life.[4]

Hence, when religion is mixed with politics to put forward a project of power, it becomes a dangerous, violent, undemocratic process that turns religion into a hate machine that attacks democracy and diversity, forbidding people's consciousness and emancipation. For instance, in contexts such as Brazil and the United States, the faithful have been prevented from thinking critically. Thus, sexist, racist, classist, xenophobic, homophobic narratives circulate from the pulpits and on social networks under the argument of religious freedom, calling into question individual and collective rights. In such contexts, religion takes precedence over any type of legislative or legal framework that protects the principle of equality. Nevertheless, what it is possible to observe so evidently nowadays emerged as a Protestant movement in the nineteenth century in the United States in defense of Christian orthodoxy, and the infallibility and the literal interpretation of the Bible, in response to modernist trends that was developing in American society of the time.

In a short book called *Fundamentalism, Terrorism and the Future of Humanity*, Boff states, the term "fundamentalism" emerged between 1910 and 1915, when a small collection of twelve booklets entitled *The Fundamentals: A Testimony to the Truth* was published. The collection refers to a movement within Christianity that gives vital importance to the infallibility or inerrancy of the Bible. In this perspective, those who do not share this religious position are not truly Christians. So, if fundamentalist groups are driven by a desire to control the socio-political landscape, it's more crucial than ever to provide education that encourages critical thinking, as Freire advocated. Due to the lack of political awareness, religious intolerance and fanaticism must be treated as impediments to dialogue and raising people's awareness, as these elements do not contribute to healthy *convivência*. Re-signifying education for critical consciousness requires an emancipatory education that helps to read reality, denouncing injustices and announcing

---

4. Garrard, *Religious*, 4.

changes. By analyzing past and present circumstances, learning from mistakes, and committing to enhance relationships, we will certainly be taking concrete steps towards transformation.

Reflecting on social responsibility amid the challenges of our time, it is crucial to first and foremost think about the various social, political, economic, cultural, and historical dimensions that affect the lives of all people and the ever-present need for a dignified existence for everyone. Dignity is about having the right to exist in ways that preserve life and our well-being, with access to clean water, food, housing, health, education, work, and the means to live a meaningful life. It is about accessing rights in society's political, social, cultural, and economic dimensions. In some ways, it is about resisting the impetus of institutions and their power structures to exclude, alienate, and violate our fundamental rights and the possibility of a dignified existence. This exclusion can permeate many aspects of one's life and will be experienced differently depending on a person's situatedness—how their intersectionality is materially manifested.[5]

Education plays a fundamental role in fostering conscientization of when these rights to a life of dignity and shared *convivência* are not being met. To address this, it is essential to encourage critical thinking and civic participation while creating public spaces for individuals to express their perspectives and refute hegemonic narratives. Fostering conscious social responsibility requires promoting social interaction, effective communication, and critical thinking. Also, recognizing and addressing the unfair power dynamics that have an impact on our communities is vital. We should work toward building more inclusive and equitable societies that value the dignity and rights of all individuals, regardless of their background or identity. To achieve this, we must prioritize social justice and human rights and reject divisive and exclusive politics that are unfortunately prevalent today, even in nations that claim religion as their raison d'être. To tackle the intricate and multifaceted obstacles that modern nations encounter regarding social responsibility requires a refined and analytical process considering

---

5. The word "intersectionality" was coined by Kimberlé Crenshaw to describe how race, class, gender, and other individual characteristics "intersect" with one another and overlap. It refers to the idea that subjectivity is constituted by multiple interrelated aspects of one's experience. See, for instance, Case, *Intersectional Pedagogy, Complicating Identity and Social Justice*. Similarly, Freire criticizes an education that does not consider the expansive understanding of the relationships between the parts and the whole, calling this a focalized view that prevents oppressed people from seeing reality critically. See *Pedagogy of the Oppressed*, 122–23.

historical, social, economic, and cultural aspects. Thus, it becomes crucial to equip people with the aptitude, expertise, and principles required to engage in democratic societies. As Henry Giroux states,

> In an age when civic culture is collapsing and a culture of compassion gives way to a culture of cruelty, it is all the more crucial to take seriously the notion that a democracy cannot exist or be defended without informed and critically engaged citizens.[6]

This is why education has a vital role to play in fighting the resurgence of nationalism, ethnic hostilities, and the use of military power intentionally against people. Schools ought to be places where students learn how to analyze the complex elements of the educational system that frequently privilege dominant viewpoints while stifling groups that it subordinates. For example, instead of avoiding heated discussions about controversial topics, educators should encourage dialogue by providing a variety of viewpoints and facts without offering an absolute response or solution. This does not mean to be neutral or hide one's position. On the contrary, not taking a position is, in essence, taking a position. It is a tacit endorsement of the unjust status quo. As Freire reminds us,

> My very presence in the school as a teacher is intrinsically a political presence, something that students cannot possibly ignore. In this sense, I ought to transmit to the students my capacity to analyze, to compare, to evaluate, to decide, to opt, to break with. My capacity to be just, to practice justice, and to have a political presence. And as a presence, I cannot sin by omission.[7]

Considering the above, educators don't just give students the facts when they teach; they must also adopt a stance that allows them to disagree, inviting them to avoid a neutral stance, which would result in an immutable reality. Furthermore, to avoid the normalization of injustices and inequalities, educators have much to contribute to advancing students' knowledge of social responsibility, encouraging them to think critically and act as citizens who can fight for a more democratic and fair future for all. Without making education meaningful, critical, and empowering, educators run the risk of creating educational spaces where individuals have no voice and are relegated to social abandonment.

---

6. Giroux, *Race, Politics, and Pandemic Pedagogy*, 127.
7. Freire, *Pedagogy of Freedom*, 90.

Social Responsibility for Planetary *Convivência*

Critical educators must design learning spaces where the primary educational objectives should foster political literacy, a sense of agency, emancipation, critical engagement, and epistemological liberation. Such an attempt challenges the ideological control of neoliberalism with its anti-intellectualism and anti-agency that sees citizens as consumers, controlled exclusively by the market. When education fails to incorporate diverse perspectives and maintain hegemonic ideologies, it becomes a tool for perpetuating injustices. The promotion of the dominant ideology may not necessarily be done overtly. It is often done through the hidden curriculum, through omission, and through de-historicizing the very curriculum one is charged to teach.

In contexts where education is reduced to a tool for reproducing societal norms, values, and power structures, individuals are likely to be socialized into accepting and perpetuating inequality. This is particularly evident in regions plagued by conflict and violence, where education systems may be manipulated to propagate ideologies that fuel animosity and division. Thus, education becomes a battleground for competing narratives, perpetuating stereotypes and contributing to a dehumanizing discourse. In such contexts, we see the depiction of what Donaldo Macedo calls a pedagogy of lies "that are shaped and supported by the interplay of the media, business interests and the academic enterprise."[8]

This worsens tensions and impedes the development of empathy and understanding, critical elements for fostering social responsibility and conviviality. For instance, in conflict-ridden areas, history textbooks may be manipulated to portray a biased narrative that deepens existing hostilities, contributing to the perpetuation of cycles of violence. This is particularly evident in societies where discrimination based on race, gender, or socioeconomic status is deeply ingrained. Howard Zinn exemplifies how traditional history education often neglects the narratives of oppressed groups, contributing to a skewed understanding of societal progress and reinforcing existing power structures when he states that "in the United States we grow up in a quiz culture, where we're rated on the basis of how many these kinds of questions we can answer."[9] So, when education does not consider the complex history and structures of power and control we are immersed in, it does not enable individuals to read reality critically and accurately. Introducing a culture of results in education is more like an anthropological

---

8. Zinn and Macedo, *Howard Zinn on Democratic Education*, 1.
9. Zinn andMacedo, *Howard Zinn on Democratic Education*, 68.

mutation in which the act of judging educational activity based on rational, ethical, and political criteria becomes guided by productivity and efficiency measures of a supposedly neutral economy/business framework.

Wendy Brown, a political theorist, discusses how neoliberal strategies undermine people's power and weaken people's agency. In her book *Undoing the Demos*, she explores the connections among neoliberalism, democracy, and citizenship. Brown argues that neoliberalism has turned citizenship into a consumer-driven activity, putting democratic principles and social justice at risk. Neoliberalism's influence on all aspects of life has quietly eroded the core values of democracy. The resulting type of citizenship is based on personal preference, competition, and self-interest, rather than shared accountability, solidarity, and engagement. This highlights the need for a renewed focus on civic engagement and citizenship.

According to Brown, neoliberalism is "the rationality through which capitalism finally swallows humanity" resulting in the normalization of sacrificing some individuals for the survival of others. She argues that as *homo oeconomicus* gains prominence over *homo politicus*, the values of citizenship centered around the common good disappear. Instead, citizens are reduced to mere investors or consumers and are forced to conform to market metrics, hindering their ability to acquire the knowledge they need for "intelligent democratic citizenship."[10] A neoliberal mindset promotes the idea that a loyal citizen is one who can withstand austerity measures and participate in a depoliticized economy. According to her, such sacrifice "may entail sudden job losses, furloughs, or cuts in pay, benefits, and pensions, or it may involve suffering the more sustained effects of stagflation, currency deflation, credit crunches, liquidity crises, and more."[11] The one who gives up his or her rights becomes a virtuous citizen who tolerates job insecurity and rights deprivation and has lower economic expectations. Brown argues that neoliberalism "integrates state and citizenship into serving the economy and morally fuses hyperbolic self-reliance with readiness to be sacrificed."[12] In other words, individuals in the neoliberal context just have to put up with the unfair conditions in which they live without complaining. Moreover, they should be grateful for what they have been given. Therefore, in such contexts, we see fragmented individuals who become

---

10. Brown, *Undoing the Demos*, 177.
11. Brown, *Undoing the Demos*, 210–11.
12. Brown, *Undoing the Demos*, 212.

weakened and unable to reject this "sacrificial citizenship." Such challenges call for a renewed focus on social responsibility and civic engagement.

For many years, scholars and theologians of liberation in Latin America such as Gustavo Gutierrez, Leonardo Boff, Franz Hinkelammert, Hugo Assmann, and Enrique Dussel have exposed the logic of oppression and exclusion at the foundation of modern societies.[13] For instance, in the book *A Idolatria do Mercado* (*The Idolatry of the Market*), Assmann and Hinkelammert address significant topics such as how economic rationality "hijacked" and functionalized essential aspects of Christianity; how "economic religion" triggered an enormous process of idolatry, which finds its most evident expression in the supposed self-regulation of market mechanisms; and how "this economic idolatry feeds on a sacrificial ideology that implies constant sacrifices of human lives."[14]

As they delve deeper into their account, they elaborate on how the act of idolizing material possessions and the twisted beliefs surrounding it within the economy ultimately results in the sacrifice of human lives. They contend that the distorted perspectives of economic procedures justify these actions. They posit that the *homo oeconomicus*, an abstract being created by the market's creators, no longer has needs, but only tastes and preferences. Once their needs are erased, concrete questions about concrete hunger, actual death, and other crucial material conditions disappear. They are no longer historical beings, but only beings with desires, faithful devotees to the gospels of profit and competition. According to the authors, people driven by desires, who uncritically follow the principles of profit and competition, lose their sense of historical significance. Thus, the authors argue that market ethics are based on a necrophilic,[15] anti-life idea that dismisses people's rootedness in history.

Paulo Freire uses the words necrophilia and biophilia[16] to address how an economically favored elite established a twisted and complex system of regulations meant to dominate and dehumanize the masses of people deemed inferior. Such systems aim to prevent everyone's innate desire to thrive by turning them into "things" or objects. According to him, oppression is necrophilic, and it is nourished by love of death. The problems

---

13. Latin American feminist theologians, including Nancy Cardoso and Geraldina Céspedes Ulloa, have offered their unique perspectives on this topic.

14. Assmann and Hinkelammert, *A Idolatria do Mercado*, 7.

15. Assmann and Hinkelammert, *A Idolatria do Mercado*, 55.

16. Freire, *Pedagogy of the Oppressed*, 58.

caused by such oppression are motivated by the sadistic selfishness of a group whose aspirations revolve around increasing their power, seizing everything and controlling everyone and, ultimately, inhibiting the creative power of individuals. More recently, Achille Mbembe, a Cameroonian historian, political theorist, and public intellectual, coined the term necropolitics to describe the use of social and political power to decide how some people may live and how some must die. In his book *Necropolitics*,[17] he theorizes the history of the modern world, which is characterized by rising racism, fascism, and nationalism, as well as militarization, hostility, and terror.

The neoliberal project reinforces oppressive behavior by continuously excluding, or only periodically including, the poor in the capitalist system. This system dominates, exploits, and demands sacrifices from individuals while simultaneously fueling their desire for consumer goods that they cannot afford. It mainly benefits those who are already privileged and disregards the rest of society. The critical view of these authors remains relevant to thinking critically about the insidious forms of consumption that have intensified in a wired world in which visible and invisible threads connect and entangle us all. Particularly in many Christian circles today, religious language has become an integral part of the structure of the capitalist system offering religious goods, such as services in the form of persuasive fundamentalist speeches, captivating marketable goods, and promises of material prosperity. The Prosperity Gospel movement has been disseminated mainly by televangelist ministries that have expanded on all continents. One of the premises of this movement is that individuals should expect to earn in proportion to what they offer. Thus, members of these churches are encouraged to claim the blessings of physical, material, and financial prosperity in this life. And if they lack any blessings, it is just a result of a lack of faith. Such thinking becomes very attractive, especially to those living in poverty, as they cling to the promises of provision, position, and power.

Amid so many seductions, however, it is necessary to question the idea that, through the rituals of consumerism, all citizens have the same access to goods. Living with a critical and conscious mindset involves more than being a consumer. For instance, in the framework of neoliberalism, education has become primarily focused on preparing students for the labor market rather than as a means of personal expansion. The educational

---

17. Mbembe, *Necropolitics*, 2019.

process is often compared to an assembly line, with strict procedures and a strong emphasis on market interests. Unfortunately, this approach can be inhumane and overly selective, promoting competition while neglecting disadvantaged groups' challenges in accessing education. This apparent subordination of educational institutions to the neoliberal economic model, in which academic quality is determined by "outcomes" and "best practices," corroborates Brown's assertion that "the saturation of higher education by market rationality has converted higher education from a social and public good to a personal investment in individual futures, futures construed mainly in terms of earning capacity."[18]

The impact of education on social structures and behaviors has been a subject of scholarly discourse for decades. In his groundbreaking work *Pedagogy of the Oppressed*, Paulo Freire elucidates how traditional education systems can inadvertently or purposely perpetuate inequality and injustice. The banking model of education, which treats students like passive information receptacles to be filled, is criticized by Freire because it perpetuates the status quo. According to him, this paradigm upholds repressive social systems and discourages critical thought. For Freire, a teacher should not teach students merely to read and write words but to read and write their world, which implies a radical reading of reality in order to intervene in it. Teachers shouldn't just teach how to decode linguistic signs but teach students how to decode the world, which should be done in collaboration. Such perception draws attention to the permanent need for ever-renewed readings of reality that it is always evolving. That's why, for him, education is always political and when people are conscious of their role as historical beings; they act to remove obstacles that restrict them from fully participating in society.

Freire underlines that any injustices a person may suffer are historically induced and not the result of natural phenomena. Therefore, to be a responsible citizen, one must stay informed on political issues, participate in public debates, and hold leaders accountable for their actions. By engaging in this way, citizens demonstrate how democracy requires the active participation of individuals in the public space, a fundamental element in addressing social injustices. An alienated person is one who does not acknowledge one's rights as a historical being and instead lets others

---

18. Brown, *Undoing the Demos*, 181. See also the author's critical analysis of what she calls the ubiquitous concept of best practice and its close cousin and predecessor benchmarking as exemplary of many features of neoliberal governance, 135–42.

determine who they are and where they belong in society. Therefore, to offer a cogent framework for consciousness, Freire encourages a conscientization process that entails working with the vocabulary and generative words pulled from people's experiences rather than being brought from the outside. Creating consciousness entails ending this cycle of alienation and generating the awareness necessary for individuals to understand themselves fully within the systems that have power over them so they can seek autonomy and emancipation.

Freire acknowledged that one of his dreams was to persuade parents, teachers, and students to think about ways they might support and exercise democracy. He believed democracy could not be defined as a political system that increases disparities, empowers the powerful, and despises weak and neglected citizens. His ideal democratic society was one that upholds its people's rights, fosters social cohesiveness, and rejects authoritarian or unjust ideologies. To him, knowledge is created through collective efforts that form politically and socially conscious people who help society advance the much-desired justice while rejecting neoliberal agendas.[19] In the current context, the market needs workers with skills to meet the new production demands of a globalized world. Thus, education within the neoliberal model aims to "train"[20] students to work in a global economy, improving their skills in a way that meets the demands of the economic model. This helps explain why civic education and students' readiness to participate in a global economy by satisfying market demands are prioritized in the neoliberal education model. As contemporary philosopher and political theorist Martha Nussbaum argues,

---

19. From the perspective of sociocultural theory, human nature is social and human beings construct knowledge in collaboration with other members of their group mediated by symbols and signs shared in culture. Thus, knowledge is contextualized and emerges out of activities and social experiences. Cultural-historical activity theory (CHAT), inspired by the work of Vygotsky and his colleagues Leont'ev and Luria, has emerged as an interdisciplinary approach that emphasizes the role of culture as a key element in understanding the interdependence between context and the mental processes of people involved in social activities. It rejects a historical-methodological approach that relies upon standardized and static procedures that tries to explain that the processes of human mind were determined by nature. See Kozulin et al., *Vygotsky's Educational Theory in Cultural Context*.

20. I am using the word train in quotation marks to highlight the difference between "to train" and "to educate." Freire opposes the word "training" because, for him, people are formed, or de-formed, but not trainable. See Freire, *Pedagogia da Tolerância*, 330.

Social Responsibility for Planetary *Convivência*

> Thirsty for national profit, nations, and their systems of education, are heedlessly discarding skills that are needed to keep democracies alive. If this trend continues, nations all over the world will soon be producing generations of useful machines, rather than complete citizens.[21]

The concept of "for-profit" education aims to limit the agency of its participants, including students and educators, preventing them from becoming critical members of their community and autonomous beings who can contribute to strengthening of democracy. As Chandra Mohanty contends,

> The role of teachers has shifted radically in this process from being educators with control over our own labor and the products of our labor to commodity producers and delivers. Correspondingly, students have become consumers of yet another commodity—education. (. . .) This is then a formula for the 'deprofessionalization' or 'proletarianization' of the professoriate.[22]

When "trained" under this model, students and educators often lack the ability to reflect critically on society's unfair arrangements, policies, values, and consumerist patterns that are ecologically unsustainable. This can result in individuals who cannot identify and address systemic issues within their society and lead to the rise of violent exclusionary political movements. Nussbaum's approach emphasizes the importance of fostering critical reflection, empathy, and ethical reasoning, which are essential for individuals to engage responsibly in a diverse and interconnected world.

From a social responsibility standpoint, the social and cultural fabric of human existence must necessarily address the struggles of those who have been historically marginalized. Issues of rights and obligations, ethical responsibilities, and collective participation are essential dimensions for a broader understanding of the cultivation of democratic values such as respect, empathy, solidarity, and basic needs for a dignified life. Unfortunately, when driven by the neoliberal agenda, education prioritizes profitability and uniformity and obstructs the realization of a critical and liberating education. So, individuals who lack the necessary skills to address social inequalities tend to foster an unwavering vision of community life.

Uncritically incorporating the culture and principles of the corporate world into schools can result in people being defined by their ability to consume and operate within the market's "irrationality" rather than focusing

---

21. Nussbaum, *Not for Profit*, 2.
22. Mohanty, *Feminism without Borders*, 180.

on their democratic participation. The emphasis on accountability in the education business model can lead to political, intellectual, and social illiteracy. As a person unequipped to read and sense the competitive corporate landscape, one loses the ability to address urgent problems of the day, as Henry Giroux contends,

> The embrace of ignorance is at the center of political life today, and reactionary forms of mass media and public pedagogy have become powerful forces of indoctrination. Civic illiteracy is the modus operandi for depoliticizing the population and disarming it of the ability to recognize, articulate, and advance its own interests.[23]

He adds that uninformed citizens, dissatisfied customers and self-centered audiences cannot hold corporate and political power accountable. Thus, the abusive and oppressive arrangements of our current contexts, including all unjust actions taken behind closed doors or in broad daylight, are malicious strategies to collapse and weaken our democracies. Education "for profit" follows the format of the banking model of education that Paulo Freire emphatically criticized. It is an attack on public education to promote the privatization bandwagon of neoliberal politics that tries to erase the skills, values, and a sense of social responsibility that enables students to be critical and engaged agents.

In a banking education model, the teacher, as the predominant subject of education, turns the learners into repositories of alienating and oppressive knowledge, giving them information that they passively receive, memorize, and repeat. When learners accept the passive role imposed on them, they fail to participate actively in their learning process or engage in critical reflection. Freire argued that the banking model approach is flawed as it views knowledge as a static commodity that can be easily transferred from one person to another. This approach hinders active participation and creativity in the learning process. To overcome the teacher-learner contradiction, Freire proposed that teachers adopt the roles of co-investigators and partners in the educational endeavor. This involves engaging with students in critical reading of their reality and promoting an actual act of liberation. Teachers can foster a more collaborative and inclusive learning environment by replacing their roles as depositor, prescriber, or domesticator.[24] From this standpoint, education is seen as the antithesis of

---

23. Giroux, *The Violence of Organized Forgetting*, 196–97.
24. Freire, *Pedagogy of the Oppressed*, 52–58.

an educational framework that is subservient to the demands of neoliberal "best practices." In various writings, Freire strongly denounces the dubious strategies of neoliberalism, asserting his opposition,

> I cannot avoid a permanently critical attitude toward what I consider to be the scourge of neoliberalism, with its cynical fatalism and its inflexible negation of the right to dream differently, to dream of utopia. My abhorrence of neoliberalism helps to explain my legitimate anger when I speak of the injustices to which the ragpickers among humanity are condemned.[25]

Neoliberal ideology has the ability to distort reality, narrow our perspective, and make us oblivious to important information. As a result, we tend to accept its bleak outlook on life passively. Its persuasive power lies in convincing us that we have no choice but to surrender to our destined fate. Freire criticizes the ethics of a neoliberal ideology based on the perversity of a world built on the foundation of exclusion and injustice where few have privileges while the vast majority is condemned to suffering and forgetfulness. He strongly believes that it's crucial for people to be knowledgeable about historical events and the socio-cultural-economic barriers that hinder their ability to live a decent life. He further proposes that individuals should analyze their reality with critical senses, keeping in mind that they have much room for improvement. By being aware of their unfinished condition, they can work toward improving their situations without falling into the trap of neoliberal fatalism. So, he proposes an ethics of solidarity that goes against the values of neoliberalism. This ethics presupposes that hope is not just stubbornness, but instead a necessary part of existence that requires anchoring in practice.[26]

In a world of political and economic turmoil, where economic and epistemological hegemony and normativity of all tones try to define and limit human subjectivity and social relations, Paulo Freire's thought remains relevant and essential. He advocated for a liberation pedagogy that prioritizes personal growth and empowerment over a pedagogy of results, emphasizing the importance of "education as a practice of freedom." In *Pedagogy of the Oppressed*, he declares that dehumanization—a concrete historical fact—is not destiny but is manufactured by the unjust order that generates violence and exclusion. It is a distortion of the vocation of becoming more fully human. The idea of striving to be more is rooted in

25. Freire, *Pedagogy of Freedom*, 22.
26. Freire, *Pedagogy of Hope*, 2.

the rejection of oppressive violence that some individuals face. It aims to achieve freedom for both those who suffer as well as those who inflict harm. The goal is to create new ways of co-existing in the world.[27]

Freire contends that it is not enough to educate some people to understand their duties and accept their responsibilities while having others denied their "right to be."[28] For him, being a person means consciously understanding one's condition and working for one's emancipation. When individuals, through a process of conscientization, become aware of their reality and recognize the obstacles that prevent them from reaching their full potential, they can resist oppression and rescue their humanity to be more fully who they desire to be. Implicit in the expression "being more" cherished by Freire is the assumption of the unfinished character of human beings and, therefore, the hopeful defense that we can build our humanity in a dignified and just manner. It is the affirmation of the possibility of freeing oneself from historical situations of oppression in the name of an experience of freedom, autonomy, and continuous becoming and unbecoming.

According to Freire, "being more" is the rejection of fatalistic discourses that try to convince individuals that changes are impossible. Being more transcends the superficiality of a pseudo-citizenship that leaves untouched the fundamental elements that threaten and make a dignified life unfeasible, and disregards alternative projects that can alter the organization of life in society so that there are no "surplus" people. Nita Freire reminds us that "being more" does not pertain to the accumulation of material wealth. Instead, it entails the capacity to broaden one's understanding of humanity itself.[29]

In this sense, to be more, one must be willing to engage in dialogue that recognizes valid feelings of anger and rebellion when life is denied, while simultaneously seeking coexistence that respects and appreciates cultural diversity. The unfinished character of human beings and the consciousness of this unfinishedness makes human beings ethically responsible for improving their individual life on the planet.[30] Moreover, it encompasses a *conscientização* process in which previously colonized minds become able to claim their rights to exist and flourish. The concept of conscientization entails an interconnected relationship between taking action and reflecting

---

27. Freire, *Pedagogy of the Oppressed*, 25–26.
28. Freire, *Pedagogy of the Oppressed*, 38.
29. Nita Freire, *Paulo Freire—Pedagogia dos Sonhos Possíveis*, 15–17.
30. Freire, *Pedagogy of Freedom*, 51–57.

on one's situation. It is a process that encourages individuals carefully to examine the historical and societal realities and dedicate themselves to making positive changes. To achieve this, people must cultivate a critical mindset, thoroughly comprehend the underlying causes, restrictions, and potential solutions to their circumstances to successfully advocate for the transformation of their contexts. According to Freire, conscientization is an essential and ongoing process of critical resistance.

Social responsibility constructed through a process of *conscientização*—the codification of marks of the culture—reveals the unavoidable rupture with the cruel system and the oppressive relations between oppressor and oppressed. Authors such as Frantz Fanon and Albert Memmi have extensively discussed the impact of Western expansion and the consequent colonization of people's minds—a colonization that persists in schools today that promote acritical education. Freire emphasizes that this is precisely why we must fight for an education that promotes democracy and liberation.[31] For critical educators, language, culture, and politics play a critical role in shaping one's life experiences. Therefore, becoming a socially responsible individual implies the capacity to denounce the reality of oppression and announce a new possibility as a conscious, autonomous, and emancipated person. The ugly reality of oppression cannot be dismissed because any attempt to suppress historical evidence of gender oppression, ethnic erasure, race struggles, economic drives, and even religious hegemony inevitably will constitute a disservice and impediment to a dignified existence. In this sense, any uncritical and naive fascination with the rhetoric of the market and its neoliberal ideals that attempt to steal the humanizing dimension of education, reducing the educational process to mere market skills, must be contested and interrupted.

Henry Giroux, writing on the relationship among education, politics, and culture, argues the need to have a critical theory and a pedagogy of citizenship education that encompasses a restructuration of a "visionary language and public philosophy that puts equality, liberty, and human life at the center of the notions of democracy and citizenship."[32] Such a critical theory and pedagogy will inevitably redefine and have an impact on the "role of the citizen as an active agent in questioning, defining, and shaping

---

31. Freire, *Pedagogy of Hope*, 176.
32. Giroux, *Teachers as Intellectuals*, 170.

one's relationship to the political sphere and the wider society" and the role of teachers as radical intellectuals.[33] Giroux attests:

> democracy cannot function without an informed citizenry. Beneath the hidden order of market-driven politics is a mode of depoliticization in which social and economic issues are removed from: the historical contexts in which they emerged; the discourse and registers of power that produced them; and ultimately reduced to utterly privatized, emotional, and personal vocabularies.[34]

Giroux maintains that education should foster a sense of agency and empowerment among citizens so they may organize themselves to resist prevailing ideologies and hierarchies of power. Therefore, creating spaces for alternatives through which students recover their agency and dignity as human beings are crucial opportunity where they can have the knowledge and courage to make changes. He says,

> Responsibility breathes politics into educational practices and suggests both a different future and the possibility of politics itself. Responsibility makes politics and agency possible, because it does not end with matters of understanding since it recognizes the importance of students becoming accountable for their ideas, language, and actions.[35]

For him, recognizing the injustices, paradoxes, and circumstances that lead to human misery is not the same as finding solutions. As a result, to teach students to assume responsibility for guiding society toward a more attainable democracy, pedagogy must provide the possibilities of understanding and acting, engaging theory and practice.

In this challenging scenario of becoming socially responsible, we must recognize that achieving this objective alone is impossible. Instead, this objective requires a joint effort with personal and collective involvement as well as democratic commitments. Classrooms can become spaces to rehearse such forms of intervention in the world through collective reflection, contestation, modification of dynamics, and levels of engagement. A comprehensive and radical understanding of social engagement must include an ethical aspect that prioritizes the flourishing and well-being of all. To achieve this in a democratic society, education should equip citizens

---

33. Giroux, *Teachers as Intellectuals*, 170.
34. Giroux, *Education and the Crisis of Public Values*, 32.
35. Giroux, *On critical Pedagogy*, 126.

with the knowledge, attitudes, and skills to make decisions aligned with democratic values and ethical principles. An educational system that encourages simplifying these complex issues without considering the strands that tie human relationships together is a discriminatory and cruel system, which treats as equals those who have not had the same opportunities and are therefore more likely to fail. Working together toward shared objectives and fostering a society that can exercise *convivência*, it is crucial for people to respect and comprehend one another.

The centrality of social responsibility for planetary *convivência* is evident in the profound impact of education on shaping individuals' perspectives, values, and actions. Traditional education models that perpetuate inequality and injustice contribute to the proliferation of conflicts and violence. However, a critical and emancipatory education offers an alternative paradigm that fosters social responsibility, empathy, and a commitment to justice. While the potential of transformative education to promote social responsibility is evident, its implementation faces various challenges. One major hurdle is the resistance from established educational systems and institutions that may be entrenched in traditional paradigms. The inertia of these systems, often resistant to change, can impede the adoption of critical and emancipatory approaches. Overcoming this resistance requires a concerted effort to reform institutional structures, curricula, and teacher formation programs. Teacher preparedness is another critical factor. Educators must be equipped with the skills and knowledge necessary to facilitate transformative learning experiences. This involves understanding the content and cultivating pedagogical approaches that encourage critical thinking, dialogue, and the exploration of diverse perspectives. Furthermore, issues of accessibility and inclusivity must be addressed and parental and community participation must also be central to any form of democratic education.

Transformative education for social responsibility should be accessible to all, regardless of socioeconomic status, gender, ethnicity, or geographic location. In many cases, marginalized communities face additional barriers to accessing quality education. Efforts to bridge these gaps are crucial for ensuring that the benefits of transformative education reach all segments of society. A nuanced understanding of cultural context is also imperative in implementing transformative education. While there are universal principles of social responsibility, the methods and content of transformative education must be tailored to each community's cultural and contextual specifics. This requires an approach that values and integrates local knowledge, histories, and experiences into the curriculum. Evaluation and assessment frameworks should be rethought to align with the goals of transformative education. Standardized testing, often criticized for promoting rote memorization and discouraging critical thinking, does not effectively address the specific needs of transformative learning experiences. Alternative assessment methods that focus on the development of critical skills, ethical reasoning, and a sense of social responsibility should be explored and integrated into the educational system.

Despite these challenges, the potential benefits of transformative education for planetary *convivência* cannot be overstated. As societies become increasingly interconnected, the need for individuals who can navigate the complexities of a diverse and globalized world becomes ever more pressing. Transformative education for social responsibility offers a pathway to cultivate the kind of engaged, critical, and socially responsible citizens essential for addressing the multifaceted challenges of our times.

4

Care-full Education
Resisting a Culture of Care-lessness

> We find that we have become brutalized by poverty not only material but poverty of mind, unable to sympathize with the pain and suffering of others. So, we isolate ourselves, harden ourselves, as if by doing so we become less susceptible or immune to pain and widespread carelessness. However, in the drive to become pain-resistant, we become more fragile and more painful to each other. Our carelessness drives us away from each other, causes the destruction of civilizations, and extinguishes the biodiversity of our planet. We are equipped with medicines, pesticides, subterfuges to preserve life when in reality we are stricken with the collective epidemic of fear, loneliness, intolerance, and life escapes us.
>
> —Abraham J. Heschel, *The Insecurity of Freedom*

THE EROSION OF CIVIL liberties, denial of climate change by governments, and violations of human rights all over the globe remind us that structural inequality and disenfranchisement have physical and emotional tolls, necessitating reflection on these issues aiming to find viable ways to restore our well-being. As the rise of an authoritarian far-right around the globe threatens the most vulnerable communities, and where constructive political change is much needed, attention to care becomes crucial. Care should be at the forefront of discussions, especially considering the current political, technological, social, and educational crisis. When institutions and infrastructures fail to approach this problem objectively, a macro perspective should be employed to critically analyze who cares and how they care, as well as who is cared for or not and why. Such reflection must consider how care is inextricably linked to systemic inequality and power structures and, thus, how care becomes a vital axis to propose radical solutions that exceed those supplied by the neoliberal lookout, which has proven insufficient in its supply of care that characterizes our present social landscape.

Moreover, when crisis and disasters are relentlessly pervasive structures through which, for some, hope becomes an unattainable utopia, and discouragement and disorientation are inevitable results, we need to make use of the hope that Freire invites us to embrace because it is precisely in the face of the impossible that we need to educate our hope. Or, as Elizabeth Povinelli describes it, we need to see care as otherwise.[1] Even if care does not entirely eradicate structural inequities and conventional beliefs about gender, race, class, sexual orientation, ableism, and so on, it can present us with an alternative. So, engaging all aspects that involve care and approaching it critically and collectively is imperative in times such as this.

Furthermore, the degradation of our ecosystem, generated by people's actions, demands an urgent need to reflect on its consequences and to propose new forms of conviviality aiming at how humans can take practical measures to care for one another, our planet, and other living beings. Sadly, after so many years, humans still have not found ways to put in place coordinated actions to change the progress of this destructive path, let alone articulate plausible considerations for future generations who deserve to live on a habitable planet. Competition and selfishness have caused us to lose touch with the natural world, leading to a lack of care. To improve our mutual understanding and enhance our ability to trust and listen to each other, we need to expand our interactions beyond our groups. We should cultivate a sense of careful attention to each other and the planet. By doing so, we can help bridge the gap that has been created and work towards a more caring and connected world.

The understanding of care conveyed in this chapter will undoubtedly be incompatible with neoliberal logic that emphasizes individuality and egoistic pursuit in which human and environmental life is being sacrificed in the name of capital accumulation. Thus, paying attention to the conflicting, disrespectful, and domineering relationships that affect the quality of

---

1. Povinelli, "The Will to Be Otherwise," 453–75.

human relationships and compromise collaborative efforts for the common good is crucial to our attention and reflection on the centrality of care. Even though the dimension of care invites us to analyze the precariousness of life established by careless attitudes in contemporary societies—making it nearly impossible to distance oneself from this macro view of care—analyzing care from a pedagogical perspective intends to underscore the crucial importance of this concept for the promotion of a pedagogy for planetary *convivência*. In addition, as the chapter aims to show, caring attitudes must be fostered in everyone, regardless of gender or sexual orientation, race, citizenship status, or religious affiliation, as well as age or living circumstances. So, by strengthening our capacity to listen to and trust one another, we will foster undivided attention to one another's needs and recognize the potential of care to improve the lives of all. Although it is outside the purview of this chapter to analyze care in detail in all its socio-political-economic facets, the chapter intends to highlight the significance of care and argue how this understanding can contribute to the promotion of planetary *convivência*.

The Need to Care and Be Cared For

One of the most fundamental aspects of our lives is the *need to care* and *be cared for*. Care is an essential part of any stage of human existence. It comprises our physical, emotional, and spiritual health, our interactions among ourselves, and our relationship with the earth and all created things in the universe. By care, we can understand the organization and daily maintenance of life, the most fundamental requirements that enable the sustainability of our existence. Because care permeates all dimensions of life, whether in caring for the body, mind, spirit, or relationships if one of these is lacking, it will undoubtedly affect the well-being of a person. Thus, care is not only a necessity to survive but a commitment to a way of being which recognizes the centrality of interdependence and relatedness among all human beings. Although we tend to relate care primarily to children or people in vulnerable situations (sick, elderly), the truth is that we all need care, and we are both caregivers and care recipients in some way or another.

Due to our society's profound unequal and patriarchal nature, care has been historically devalued and traditionally associated with women. Understood as a moral obligation and a woman's work, it is linked to the domestic sphere and frequently related to unpaid or underpaid caring labor. Such a view has been challenged by some prominent feminists who have challenged the androcentric and essentialist view of care. For instance, political scientist Joan Tronto and feminist educator Berenice Fisher argue that this hierarchy causes fragmentation in the care process, harming the care objective and placing caregivers in low-power positions.[2] The authors contend that a lower standing is frequently accorded when a profession is connected to caregiving, such as nursery, teaching, or childcare.

Understanding care as a fundamental principle and requirement for contemporary society is an unavoidable task that we must undertake if we want to reject such a patriarchal view of care that essentializes the role of women or any specific groups for that matter. These hierarchies, which are molded by a complex interplay of elements, including race, gender, class, nationality, and other intersecting identities, frequently lead people to marginalization, discrimination, and violence if they deviate from accepted standards. Their lives become more vulnerable and precarious precisely because they do not fit within the established frameworks of recognition and care. Therefore, we must develop an ethic of care that recognizes the responsibility of all people to care and being cared for. We must create means to promote systemic changes that genuinely place the care of others and collective life at the center of our concerns, and we must foster a future where our young people can live more compassionately. Compassion must always be preceded by empathy. However, such empathy must enable solidarity to confront precarity and challenge practices to go beyond paternalistic charity.

As philosopher Vrinda Dalmya argues, empathetic "care" can become a moment of resistance by grounding political solidarity for structural change. In contrast, paternalistic care distorts the functioning of affection and empathy, and further consolidates colonial hierarchies.[3] Thus, in light of Dalmya's arguments, when communities provide charity and remedial assistance without addressing the root causes of injustice and social unrest, empathy—a crucial component of care—becomes compromised reinforcing existing patterns of domination. Thus, acknowledging the importance of empathy is consistent with both the precariousness and the "politicization" of care ethics.

Care, in this perspective, requires intelligence both to deal with overcoming the understanding that places care exclusively in the scope of

2. Tronto and Fisher. "Toward a Feminist Theory of Caring," 36–54.
3. Daylmia, "Vulnerability," 72.

subjectivity—and thus away from an intellectual and rational understanding of what it entails—and intelligence to perceive problems and change behavior patterns so that guarantee the survival of people and the planet. From this outlook, relationships characterized by love, tenderness, affection, responsibility, dedication to the other, and preservation of life are palpable ways care becomes a concrete reality. However, the lack of care is self-evident if one observes our current contexts, whether in interpersonal relationships or natural calamities. It reveals our little consideration for one another and even less for the environment. Therefore, it is undeniably vital to examine the kind of care we provide, or should provide, for one another; the care we dispense to the earth—our generous Mother—and the care we offer to other living beings if we want to preserve life on the planet in this dramatic moment when the planet's limits of self-regeneration are being squeezed.

The idea of mutual dependency and vulnerability and the ethical duty we must take on for the spirit of coexistence to endure is brought about by realizing and accepting the primacy of care in our lives and human interactions. In this regard, it's essential to acknowledge human frailty, paying attention to the demand for attitudes and dispositions that view care as a crucial component of interpersonal relationships. Additionally, the ontological aspect of care and how it affects human relationships enables us to view differences not as insurmountable obstacles but as opportunities to extend our interactions outside of our groups, enhancing our ability to communicate effectively with one another and to listen to and trust others.

The definitions of being attentive and being dedicated to others are two concepts that are intricately interwoven and call for a collective reimagining of care as a political response to challenge structural inequalities and to confront the normalization of violence and carelessness as we have witnessed during government responses to the coronavirus pandemic in the United States and Brazil. Political carelessness and social indifference, as well as the lack of adequate responses to the coronavirus pandemic, were evident in the relativization of the impact of the pandemic and the trivialization of its effects on the lives of most of the population by these governments. As Heschel reminds us, in this chapter's epigraph, when we are incapable of feeling other people's anguish and suffering, civilizations are destroyed, and the planet's biodiversity is lost. We become infected by a pandemic of indifference, negligence, contempt, and intolerance, thus becoming brutalized by a poverty of the mind.

A Pedagogy for Planetary *Convivência*

In the book *Precarious Life: The Power of Mourning and Violence*, Judith Butler, a philosopher and gender studies scholar, makes a central claim that life is inherently precarious and vulnerable.[4] Butler argues that precarity helps us understand how vulnerability is unequally distributed, with some people being seen as disposable and having less access to resources due to factors like neoliberal policies and war. Precarity exposes the fragile and necessary dimensions of our interdependency. According to Butler, every political effort to manage societies, whether openly stated or not, involves strategically distributing precarity, often resulting in an unfair distribution of such precarity. This distribution of precarity is what decides whose life is grievable and worthy of protection and whose life is ungrievable, or marginally or episodically grievable, and so, in that sense, already lost in part or in full, and therefore less worthy of protection and sustenance. Furthermore, Butler argues that systemic biases, entrenched structural inequalities and the normalization of violence perpetuate unequal distribution and precarity of certain lives in our world.[5] Butler considers what links us morally to alterity, understood as those whose lives are marred by precarity, is not a given; it depends on our capacity to see the threatened humanity in the Other. The issue of the Other's depiction in our media-driven age thus becomes even more difficult. In many cases, the media either forbids us from seeing the Other or depicts them in a way that hinders our ability to identify with them. For the author, the depiction of alterity can be used either to humanize or dehumanize someone, recognize our moral and ethical obligations to the Other, or serve as a reason for eradicating them.

Butler's claims prompt us to consider why particular lives are deemed valuable and deserving of care while others are left vulnerable and precarious. Thus, if the distribution of care is not only based on inherent value or worthiness but is deeply enmeshed in power structures and norms that shape our social fabric, it leads us to reflect critically on how we care and how we are cared for. If we accept Butler's analysis, we should also accept the call for a collective reimagining of care as a political response to challenge these inequalities. We must recognize that a politics of care should strive to identify and address the specific vulnerabilities faced by marginalized communities rather than perpetuating the status quo. Therefore, taking Butler's analysis beyond the scope of individual acts of care or neglect,

---

4. Butler, *Precarious Life*.
5. Butler. "Vida Precária," 13–33.

we must look at the broader systemic forces that perpetuate the carelessness mindset and promote, instead, a perspective that fosters a more empathetic and compassionate approach to care.

Looking at Butler's analysis through the lens of care, we can draw parallels with Joan Tronto's ideas presented in *Caring Democracy: Markets, Equality, and Justice*.[6] In this book, she argues that care should be the central concern of democratic political life and offers a political perspective on feminist care theory. The book examines how neoliberal political ideology treats the market as the whole of democracy, neglects caring responsibilities, and constrains freedom and equality in undemocratic ways. Tronto emphasizes the need to reassess our fundamental values and commitments from a care perspective, arguing that we cannot prioritize economic life and the means of production while disregarding how gender, race, class, and market forces misallocate caring responsibilities. Thus, concerns about caring for ourselves and others should shape our view of the economy, politics, and institutions such as schools and families. The author argues that for a democracy to function properly, it is essential to ensure all community members have access to the resources needed to provide and receive care. This involves acknowledging that caring for others is a collective social responsibility with certain obligations. She emphasizes the importance of recognizing and addressing these responsibilities to promote a healthy and functioning society, declaring,

> To envision a society as democratic and caring is to envision a society whose account of justice balances how the burdens and joys of caring are equalized so as to leave every citizen with as much freedom as possible. Such a vision requires that citizens see clearly how they care with others, that is, how they think about responsibilities for care.[7]

Recognizing and redistributing care is crucial in combating social injustice and promoting inclusion, especially considering the growing disparities in income, health, and education. According to the author, our ability to care for ourselves and others will only increase if we dare to admit that we need and will benefit from recognizing the vast network of affectionate relationships that give meaning to our lives. Tronto asserts,

---

6. Tronto, *Caring Democracy*.
7. Tronto, *Caring Democracy*, 46.

> There is a way to turn our world around. It requires us to recommit to caring for ourselves and others by accepting and rethinking our caring responsibilities and providing sufficient resources for care. If we are able to do this, then we will be able to enhance levels of trust, reduce levels of inequality, and provide real freedom for all.[8]

The relational and cooperative aspects of care underscore the interdependence and shared responsibility in care relationships, with all the contradictions and ambivalences. Therefore, it is crucial and pressing to contemplate these inconsistencies and find ways to address the multifaceted and complex challenges that endanger the lives of especially vulnerable individuals. When we acknowledge the influence of social structures that result in inequality and take objective steps to provide necessary support, we will undoubtedly strengthen our democracy.

It is important to recognize that caring for the planet is not just about humans, but also about all living beings. This means we need to implement effective practices and policies that protect and restore our ecosystems for present and future generations. By understanding the interconnection between all living things, we can take urgent action to preserve and restore the planet's health and biodiversity.

Pope Francis invites us in his encyclical *Laudato Si—Caring for our Common Home* to nurture a "passion for the care of the world,"[9] which implies assuming our responsibility for taking care of one another and the Earth. He reminds us that "a true ecological approach always becomes a social approach; it must integrate questions of justice in debates on the environment, so as to hear both the cry of the earth and the cry of the poor."[10] The depletion of natural resources in forests and rivers has a greater impact on vulnerable populations who rely on them for survival. When a country destroys its forests, pollutes its rivers, and exploits its natural resources for profit, it not only harms its vulnerable populations who depend on these resources for survival but also causes ecocide that puts all other forms of life at risk. This serious issue needs urgent attention and action to prevent further damage to our planet.

The impact of ecological disasters on different human groups within the same society varies significantly. Destruction of forests or water contamination can lead to diseases and precarious living conditions for some

---

8. Tronto, *Caring Democracy*, 182.
9. Papa Francisco, *Laudato Si'*, 216.
10. Papa Francisco, *Laudato Si'*, 49.

groups more than others. When vulnerable communities face a disproportionate burden of pollutants and other hazards due to their geographic location, income, or race, it constitutes an environmental injustice. To achieve environmental justice, it is crucial that individuals have equal opportunities to participate in decisions that affect their environment. This entails having access to a safe, healthy, productive, and sustainable environment, as well as equitable access to clean air, water, and land for all, regardless of their income or race. Therefore, when addressing care-related matters, it's essential to acknowledge the voices of those who are affected the most by its absence.

From this standpoint, it's crucial to recognize the interconnectedness between economics, society, and the environment to understand the significance of the matter. Pope Francis advocates for an all-encompassing approach to environmental issues, which he calls "integral ecology." To effectively address ecological problems and demonstrate genuine concern for our planet, it is essential to have a comprehensive understanding of all the factors that contribute to sustaining life on Earth. To this end, education certainly plays a key role in promoting caring attitudes towards the environment and its inhabitants, as we continue the quest to repair our broken world and relationships.

Rescuing the Role of Care in Education

In many social institutions, especially in educational environments where the emphasis on success, competition, and material achievement reduces educational experiences to a mere productivity line, it is crucial to recognize and accept the centrality of caring. When care is forgotten or denied, it reveals a more profound social malaise. Understanding the centrality of care in educational settings can help us resist the fragmentation of care or its gendered character and the urgent need to reconnect with our deeply held human values.

Education must involve consideration for everything that exists and lives. We educate people to think critically and creatively, with an eye toward a career and a good quality of life, but most of the time, we neglect to educate people to be responsible and care for the future of the planet and humanity. An education that does not include care as an educational principle is alienated and even irresponsible. Without compassion and care, we cannot ensure a sustainable future for our civilization that allows the planet to maintain its vitality, its ecosystem balance, and a feasible future for humankind. We are beings of connectedness; we rely on one another; we yearn to belong; we long for love, and we also need care to thrive. Although we would not have survived if we had not been cared for, due to an increasingly individualistic and individualizing way of life, we have grown distant from attitudes of care. Because of this, we must recuperate the dimension of care in our relationships that can protect us from the attitudes and actions that dehumanize one another and keep us apart.

Nell Noddings, a well-known educational philosopher, has significantly advanced our understanding of caring as a crucial component of teaching and learning. Her educational philosophy is founded on the notion that caring should be the main subject of moral education because it is a fundamental aspect of human nature. According to Noddings, care is not only an essential human need, but also an essential educational need.[11] Building caring relationships is a crucial aspect of promoting ethical behavior. For Noddings, teachers have the responsibility to create such relationships with their students to facilitate their growth and development. This can be achieved by setting an example of compassion and cultivating a loving environment that fosters trusting relationships. By taking an interest in the lives and well-being of their students, teachers promote a safe and encouraging learning environment that inspires the development of compassionate attitudes.

The fundamental basis of compassion and caring is empathy. Caring and compassion without empathy can sound hollow, devoid of the depth and resonance required for real human connection and support. Beyond flimsy gestures or token demonstrations of sorrow, empathy enables us to see and feel the experiences of others, establishing a sense of interconnectedness and understanding. Empathy is putting yourself in someone else's shoes. It means stripping away what we have, our concepts and prejudices, our worldview and the certainties we carry, and being ready to listen carefully to others. Empathy is putting on the lens of love and respect for people and their stories, especially those who are silenced or ignored. In our increasingly interconnected society, empathy helps us close gaps in knowledge, dismantle obstacles to prejudice and discrimination, and foster a heightened feeling of empathy among society at larger. However, in order to incorporate empathy into conversations about compassion and caring, we must first recognize its essential value and actively work to foster

---

11. Noddings, *Caring: A Relational Approach to Ethics & Moral Education.*

empathy in both in ourselves and others. To understand the viewpoints and experiences of others around us, we must be willing to listen intently, put judgment aside, and embrace vulnerability.

Another philosopher and theorist, Virginia Held, underscores the importance of care ethics in education. As a renowned philosopher who has published a great deal on care ethics, her writings have had an impact on the growth of feminist ethics and care ethics. One of Held's most important contributions to the field is her pedagogical framework for cultivating care in communities and schools. She strongly believes that care is an essential aspect of human life, necessary for both individual and societal well-being. Held defines care as encompassing qualities such as attentiveness, responsibility, competence, and responsiveness.[12] She suggests that communities and institutions create an environment that promotes the adoption of caring attitudes and behaviors. Held's educational framework for promoting care consists of three main components: caring attitudes, caring activities, and caring connections. These components work together to establish a compassionate atmosphere that benefits both individuals and society.

Although Held offers valuable insights on the connection between care and education, her emphasis on individuals tends to disregard the broader structural and systemic influences that contribute to the absence of care in schools and communities. While promoting supportive attitudes, behaviors, and relationships is essential, addressing systemic socioeconomic challenges, such as poverty, injustice, and prejudice, which often undermine supportive relationships and practices, is equally vital. Therefore, promoting care in schools and communities requires a comprehensive approach considering human and systemic factors.

The Care Manifesto

Andreas Chatzidakis and his co-authors present a unique perspective on education in their book *The Care Manifesto*.[13] They advocate for an educational system that prioritizes empathy, well-being, and holistic development. By emphasizing the importance of compassion, the authors urge policymakers to shift away from individualistic and market-driven approaches and instead adopt a care-centered approach to education. Their insightful ideas broaden our understanding of what it means to care and

12. Held, *The Ethics of Care*, 29–43.
13. Chatzidakis et al., *The Care Manifesto*.

encourage us to rethink traditional educational practices. They encourage us to cultivate inclusive and engaging learning environments that prioritize students' growth and well-being, demonstrating the importance of prioritizing care in educational practices. One of their recommendations is for educational institutions to give importance to the emotional needs of students and create environments that encourage emotional literacy, empathy, and self-care. Educators should have a knowledge of their students' emotional needs to provide practical guidance and support during challenging times. By integrating emotional well-being in educational approaches, nurturing environments can be established to foster student development.

The Care Manifesto stresses that care is not just an act of kindness, but a vital ethical and political action. This perspective urges educators to consider the broader social and political aspects of care in the context of education and to analyze power relations, inequalities, and differences that exist in educational systems. By adopting a care-focused approach, educators can encourage equality, inclusion, and social justice and strive to create a just and impartial learning environment. This involves embracing care as a core value, promoting emotional well-being, acknowledging care as an ethical and political action, promoting collaboration, and integrating care education to create dynamic and transformative educational settings.

In educational settings, collaboration is crucial for ensuring proper care. It involves the active involvement of all stakeholders, including students, parents, administrators, support staff, and educators. Collaborative care approaches can foster a sense of community, shared responsibility, and interpersonal support in educational environments. This perspective promotes the formation of partnerships and networks that prioritize care, enabling everyone to contribute to the growth and well-being of students.

Taking a critical education perspective, the idea of care challenges conventional views on teaching and learning. It highlights the significance of nurturing empathetic and compassionate individuals who can effectively navigate the intricacies of the world. This approach motivates students to scrutinize power structures, social injustices, and ethical obligations, while also promoting empathy and inclusivity. Within this educational framework, care entails rejecting the traditional education approach and embracing a liberating, transformative, and dialogical pedagogy. Understanding human vulnerability and paying attention to the need for attitudes and dispositions that consider caring a vital component of human relationships is essential for building a paradigm of religious education aimed at planetary *convivência*. In this care-centered approach, educators must prioritize their students' holistic development and well-being, empowering them to become compassionate and caring people.

Care, understood as an ethical responsibility, needs to become one of the priorities in educational environments. Caring for others involves demonstrating genuine concern for their well-being, especially those most vulnerable, and such involvement will be impossible without the ability to empathize. Such careful provision must stem from our unwavering solidarity with them. Individuals—who, consciously or anonymously, in their own time and place, have walked against the grain of individualistic and self-centered interests—have proven that we can live our lives caring about others and their struggles, thereby helping to ease their pain and suffering.[14] When we are moved by such empathy and compassion, we can recognize the intrinsic dignity and wholeness of every human being. Furthermore, when we acknowledge our vulnerability and mutual dependence, we can value the attitudes and dispositions of the mind and heart and recognize care as a crucial component of human interactions. We then create space for the spirit of conviviality to develop within and through our relationships.

The Spirituality of Care

The theme of care is important not only in interpersonal relationships but also in relationships with the environment. The catastrophic deterioration that the Earth is undergoing, evident in both the degradation and destruction of nature and the scarcity in which two-thirds of humanity lives, prompts Leonardo Boff[15] to look for a means of addressing this dire situation.

Among several books in which Boff addresses his ecological concerns, I selected two in which he deals specifically with the dimension of care. These books published in Portuguese, *Cuidado Necessário* and *Saber Cuidar: ética do humano, compaixão pela terra*,[16] offer valuable insights

---

14. The list of such exceptional human beings is vast, but we can mention names such Martin Luther King, Jr, Madre Teresa, Dom Hélder Camara, Sojourner Truth, Oscar Romero, Harriet Tubman, Desmond Tutu, among so many others.

15. Leonardo Boff is a professor emeritus at the State University of Rio de Janeiro and the author of more than 100 books addressing themes such as Ecology, Care, Ethics, Globalization, and Spirituality.

16. Boff, *Saber Cuidar: ética do humano, compaixão pela terra* and *O Cuidado Necessário* (English translation: *Essential Care—An Ethics of Human Nature*).

into our deteriorating context and our sensitive spiritual understanding in response to those challenges.

Boff has been writing about ecology and the planet's imminent collapse for decades and has insisted on the need for humankind to live in ways to reverse such a situation. According to him, the reversal of this situation will only be possible with the configuration of a new paradigm that can guide the meaning of our lives based on three premises, namely, a better relationship with the Earth, a new social pact between people, and a social agreement that respects and safeguards everything alive.[17] Although mainly dealing with the same topics, the two aforementioned books each present nuanced perspectives that complement each other. If we only pay attention to what the titles suggest, *Necessary Care* and *Knowing How to Care*, we could infer that *recognizing* that care is necessary is insufficient because such recognition does not automatically imply that we *know how to care*. Therefore, this perception reinforces the importance of learning how to care, which implies an a priori unlearning the inculcated individualistic ways of being in the world and with others.

Boff describes the nature, importance, and implications of care in human relationships, for our spirituality, and our relationship with the Earth, declaring that the issue of care serves as both a critique of our agonizing civilization and an inspiring principle for a new paradigm of conviviality.[18] Thus, understanding that human life would be inconceivable without relations of care implies an attentiveness to the ways conflict, disrespect, and domination—among others—affect the quality of human relationships and compromise collaborative efforts to work for the common good. Boff defines care as solicitude, dedication, and concern for the other and the environment, drawing from the definition elaborated by the German philosopher Martin Heidegger,[19] for whom the ultimate meaning of human existence lies in *Dasein*, meaning, *being-in-the-world-with-the-other*. In this context, the very identity of the human is built on coexistence and interrelationship. Care is at the base of this perception, understood as solicitude, dedication, and concern for the other. Heidegger's thought is based on his

---

17. Boff, *Saber Cuidar*, 17–18.
18. Boff, *Saber Cuidar*, xi.
19. Heidegger, *Being and Time*. In this book, the author dedicates part of his studies to the understanding of Being, defining the term Dasein (being-there or being-there-in-the-world), which concerns the person with the world. For Heidegger, the ultimate meaning of human existence lies in its *being-in-the-world-with-the-other*.

reading of Higino's fable in which Cora, Jupiter, and Earth argue to give the human being a name that would forever reveal a unique way of being.

> Once when 'Care' was crossing a river, she saw some clay; she thoughtfully took up a piece and began to shape it. While she was meditating on what she had made, Jupiter came by. 'Care' asked him to give it spirit, and he gladly granted. But when she wanted her name to be bestowed upon it, he forbade this, and demanded that it be given his name instead. While 'Care' and Jupiter were disputing, Earth arose and desired that her name be conferred on the creature, since she had furnished it with part of her body. They asked Saturn to be their arbiter, and he made the following decision, which seemed a just one: 'Since you, Jupiter, have given it spirit, you shall receive that spirit at its death; and since you, Earth, have given its body, you shall receive its body. But, since 'Care' first shaped this creature, she shall possess it as long as it lives. And because there is now a dispute among you as to its name, let it be called 'homo', for it is made out of *humus* [earth].[20]

According to Heidegger, caring is an attitude that involves two completely interconnected meanings: attention and dedication to the other. The person who knows how to care is attentive to the needs of others. Boff uses this definition to develop his proposal for essential care as a fundamental means to deal with our severe global crisis. Boff claims that Heidegger is the philosopher who best-understood care's fundamental significance and noted the ontological dimension of care and its implications for society. Boff states that caring means shaping our lives according to the ethos of care. In this sense, care is closely connected with an attitude of love, kindness, and cordial relationship that seeks to protect personal, social, and environmental reality.

Care is the antithesis of neglect. Care is an attitude rather than a mere action. Care stands for a mindset of engagement, accountability, and emotional investment in the other. In this sense, care is a way of being, a *modus operandi* of the person in the world and with others. Because it involves recognizing the interdependence of all creatures, caring is crucial to advancing social justice and equity. Because we are all interconnected with each other and the natural environment, our actions impact the well-being of humans and more-than-humans. Therefore, caring implies being responsible for the well-being of all. With regard to human beings, this care and compassion must be directed primarily toward oppressed and disadvantaged

---

20. Boff, *Essential Care*, 21–22.

people, which implies fighting to eradicate the causes of their oppression. This involvement requires identifying and addressing the structures of privilege and power that underpin inequality and promote social and economic injustice. It demands respecting the intrinsic value of every living thing and working to build a more just and equal society. Thus, care means simultaneously working for a more equitable and sustainable relationship with the natural world and developing a deep empathy and compassion for others. And it is only when we are emotionally invested that we begin to feel responsible for humans and more-than-humans and can offer them the attention they deserve. Care for and with is an indispensable aspect of human relationships. From the moment we are born until our last breath, we will always rely on someone's care to support us, comfort us, accept us and accompany us as we navigate the intricacies of life.

According to Boff, care only materializes if a spiritual revolution makes us sensitive to solidarity, cooperation, compassion, and justice toward others and the Earth. Such spirituality is what can root us when our contemporary society tries to uproot us. Therefore, if we agree that care is a vital part of ourselves and that we are experiencing a shortage of care as a society, we must educate ourselves on how to care and revitalize its centrality in our interactions. As humans, we possess both emotional intelligence (feelings, affection, and tenderness) and intellectual intelligence (logic) that enable us to take care of ourselves, others, and the environment. It is a mistake to prioritize or suppress one over the other. Boff claims that because people have prioritized reason above emotion, they have seriously harmed the earth's system. To prevent further harm, Boff suggests that we should prioritize *pathos*,[21] that is, the profound capacity to feel and be empathetic, the emotional connections that allow us to value people and situations, instead of favoring reason over emotions.

The notion of divine pathos is the most important theological legacy of Abraham Heschel. The divine love and concern with the deeds of the human condition are the strongest echo of biblical prophecy. According to Heschel, pathos accentuates the divine love for God's creation and the divine interest in human affairs. Therefore, the category of pathos, when taken as a starting point to think about the presence of God in the world, opens the doors to the possibility of understanding the divine passion, involvement, attentiveness, and concern for God's children and creation. God's love is not a concept; it is a force, a presence, a crossing, an experience that makes

---

21. Boff, *Saber Cuidar*, 198.

life expand and unfold. And according to Heschel, "it implies a constant concern and involvement; it is conceived as an emotional engagement."[22] Taking care of things and people implies a deep feeling of respect, involvement, and *acolhimento* (embrace).

Although every individual possesses the capacity to love, care, show compassion, and provide support, these virtues need to be nurtured to grow stronger and not weaken. Care demands a paradigm shift as the structuring axis of the praxis for planetary *convivência*. As Boff contends, instead of accepting the conquest paradigm, we must replace it with the care paradigm. Although political, economic, and structural changes are necessary, they alone are insufficient to make care possible, especially in a capitalist society.

Therefore, we also need to include a critical education. In that case, we need to prioritize educating new generations about how to care for each other, be responsible, and act with care and compassion toward others. This means treating people with love, respect, and kindness and creating *vínculos de ternura* (tenderness bonds). Such attitudes should be grounded in ethical and spiritual values that help us comprehend our place on Earth as beings existing in the vastness of the universe's beauty, greatness, and generosity.

Taking Care of Each Other

In a world where hatred and violence are encouraged and new forms of genocides emerge before our very eyes without any firm outcry from society, the parable of the Good Samaritan text (Luke 10: 25–36) shows the centrality of compassion in Jesus' pedagogy. Reflecting on this parable from the care perspective may bring us new insights into how to be in solidarity with God's creation, including humans and more-than-humans.

Within the Christian tradition, God is understood as a caring God who instructs God's people to love others, showing them mercy and compassion. The instruction to love applies not only to God and fellow companions, as we read in Deut 6:5 and Lev 19:18.[23] But also includes those who belong to different ethnic groups or even those considered enemies, as appears in Matt 5:43–45 "You have heard that it was said, 'You shall love

---

22. Heschel, *The Prophets*, 10.

23. Deuteronomy 6:5 "You shall love the Lord your God with all your heart, and with all your soul, and with all your might" and Leviticus 19:18, "You shall not take vengeance or bear a grudge against any of your people, but you shall love your neighbor as yourself: I am the Lord."

your neighbor and hate your enemy.' But I say to you: Love your enemies and pray for those who persecute you, so that you may be children of your Father in heaven, for he makes his sun rise on the evil and on the good and sends rain on the righteous and on the unrighteous."[24]

In our response to God's love, care, and compassion, we are instructed to reciprocate, to be prepared to love, and to receive love from others. These essential values, also referred to as the "golden rule," are sought after and practiced in other major religions. So, independent of our faith traditions, we are called to love and show compassion for all human beings and all creation as the Loving Creator cares for us.

For Christians, Jesus is a radical example who embodies genuine care and compassion and models to his disciples how they should live their lives. Jesus cared for the subjugated people excluded by the ruling power, the despised, and the rejected by society's ruling elites, even when his actions implied standing against the unmatched power of the Roman Empire. Jesus, as a member of an agrarian culture, was aware of the politics and economic powers that governed his context, and indeed, his teachings reflected that social-cultural context in both his denouncements and announcements.

Although the economic system during Jesus' time cannot be directly compared to the complex systems in place today, it's impossible to deny that they share similar foundations. In both cases, a small group of individuals reap the benefits while the majority struggle to live with dignity. According to esteemed New Testament scholar William Herzog, it's important for contemporary readers to consider the social and cultural contexts in which the biblical texts, specifically the parables, were written. In his book, *Parables as Subversive Speech: Jesus as Pedagogue of the Oppressed,* Herzog examines studies of ancient societies and interpretation of parables that explore the financial, military, and religious structures of first-century Rome. Herzog believes Jesus acted as a pedagogue for the oppressed and utilized parables to provide social analysis and theological reflection in a world plagued by social injustices. According to Herzog, using parables was essential to Jesus' liberation ministry.[25]

One of Jesus' paradigmatic teachings is exhibited in the Gospel of Luke 10:25–37, often called the Parable of the Good Samaritan. Herzog's analysis doesn't cover this parable, but his idea of Jesus as a pedagogue of

---

24. All scriptural passages are from the New Revised Standard Version (NRSV) of the Bible.

25. Herzog, *Parables as Subversive Speech.*

the oppressed provides valuable insights to analyze the parable of the Good Samaritan. This parable is famous for its message of aiding strangers, even those we may perceive as adversaries. Typically, it is interpreted as instructing us to love our neighbors, a fundamental Christian principle. Furthermore, the parable encourages us to adopt the Samaritan way of helping the sick, impoverished, and foreign individuals.

While I will not delve into the historical context that set apart Jews and Samaritans, it suffices to say that there were notorious hostilities between them (see John 4:9; 8:48). Upon initial examination of these first verses of the Parable of the Good Samaritan, one can easily discern the prevalent theme of compassion throughout the text. I want to take a slightly different approach and read this parable from the perspective of care. I want to argue how Jesus adopts a pedagogical approach that challenges conventional beliefs and social norms, urging his audience to transcend prejudices and embrace genuine care for others.

The passage begins with a question posed by the interpreter of the Law to Jesus, asking, "Teacher, what shall I do to inherit eternal life?" (Luke 10: 25). This question prompts Jesus to delve deeper into the nature of care and love, as he often did when addressing spiritual matters. The Law expert's query echoes the traditional Jewish concern with righteousness and salvation, seeking clarification on the requirements for eternal life. In his response, Jesus artfully employs a pedagogical approach, turning the question back to the Law expert, encouraging his active engagement and reflection on his understanding of the Law in the hope that he might see things in a new way. Then the interlocutor answers Jesus by quoting the Scriptures. In the sequence, the interpreter of the Law, wanting to justify himself, asks Jesus a second question: "Who is my neighbor?" (v. 29). Then Jesus begins to tell the story of the Samaritan traveler in response to his inquiry (vv. 30–36). After ending the story, following his dialogical pedagogy, Jesus asks, "Which of these three do you think was a neighbor?" He answered: "The one who used mercy on him." Jesus concludes with an instruction: "Go and do likewise" (v. 37).

The story has been the subject of numerous scholarly interpretations exploring the nuances of these characters. Some authors have drawn parallels to the broader human experience by stating how the man who fell victim to robbery displays the vulnerability and unpredictability of life, where unforeseen circumstances can abruptly alter one's path. The priest and Levite, as religious figures, show the challenges individuals face in reconciling professional roles and moral obligations. Their reluctance to assist the injured man could be seen as a conflict between duty and compassion, a dilemma that resonates with people from all walks of life. The Samaritan's act of compassion challenges societal norms and stereotypes. His character introduces the theme of empathy transcending cultural and social boundaries, highlighting the potential for humanity to break free from prejudices and extend a helping hand, even in the face of adversity, reminding us of the transformative power of empathy. While all of these explanations are insightful and helpful in understanding Jesus' message, I want to focus on the actions—or lack thereof—of the characters themselves: a man who was robbed and left half-dead on the side of the road; two religious leaders who saw the injured man, but chose not to act; and, a Samaritan, considered a social outcast, but who stopped and acted by providing genuine care to the injured man. From the point of view of action, we could infer that a crucial aspect of Jesus' teaching in this passage could be an emphasis on action.

From this perspective, it matters not why the priest and Levite, who held religious positions of authority and represented the religious establishment of their day, chose not to act. What matters most is their inaction and, thus, their failure to demonstrate care. The man who was wounded and traumatized by violence could not move, could not act due to his pain. The Samaritan, on the other hand, the one who acts, moves toward the man to offer practical assistance, guaranteeing that the injured man receives appropriate care and ensures ongoing care even after he leaves. This resonates with the Letter of James, where the author emphasizes the connection between faith and deeds, stating that "faith by itself, if it is not accompanied by action, is dead" (James 2:17).

The parable of the Good Samaritan imparts a powerful lesson about the importance of care and emphasizes that genuine care cannot exist without acts of justice and solidarity. Jesus urges the interpreter of the Law to go beyond simply adhering to religious practices and instead embrace care that is founded on acting and bringing about systemic change. The Samaritan's unexpected actions call for introspection and inspire a more profound comprehension of love and empathy. By emphasizing the significance of actions over words or status, Jesus underscores the universal call to care for others genuinely. He challenges preconceived notions and religious norms that are bound by social and religious restrictions, prioritizing compassion and care instead. This narrative is a timeless reminder of the complexities inherent in human interactions and the perpetual quest for ethical rectitude. In essence, the story not only unfolds as a compelling narrative but also serves as a profound reminder of the shared human experience, inviting reflection on the actions, motivations, and capacity for compassion in the face of life's trials and the transformative power of compassionate action. Through the lens of Latin American liberation theology, care emerges as a transformative force, rooted in solidarity, justice, and love for the marginalized. This passage continues to resonate in Latin American Christianity, inspiring and stimulating believers to embrace care that fosters liberation and authentic human connection. Gustavo Gutierrez, a Dominican priest and one of the forerunners of liberation theology, expresses this concept eloquently,

> The parable of the Good Samaritan ends with the famous inversion which Christ makes of the original question. . . .When everything seemed to point to the wounded man in the ditch on the side of the road, Christ asked, "which of these three do you think was neighbor to the man who fell into the hands of the robber?" The neighbor was the Samaritan who approached the wounded man and made him his neighbor. The neighbor, as has been said, is not the one whom I encounter in my path, but rather the one in whose path I place myself, the one whom I approach and actively seek.[26]

Gutierrez has given us a thought-provoking perspective on caring for others. Care must emerge from the disposition of our hearts. It emphasizes the importance of empathy and putting ourselves in the shoes of those we care for. To care for someone effectively, we must first acknowledge and recognize their needs, which implies making others and their needs visible.

Leonardo Boff maintains that we need to see like the Samaritan, who "sees with the eyes of the heart for he fills himself with compassion."[27] If we prioritize the well-being of those more in need than ourselves, we can show genuine compassion. Compassionate care involves setting aside our wants and focusing on the needs and well-being of others. It means empathizing with the other person's pain and doing what we can to help alleviate it. As Boff reiterates, "Compassion means to assume the same 'passion' of the other."[28] Extending one's shoulders and hands is a kind gesture of providing support and showing care. As Boff highlights, the Samaritan didn't ask, as Jesus' interlocutor did, "Who is my neighbor?" It was up to the Samaritan to

---

26. Gutierrez, *A Theology of Liberation*, 113.
27. Boff, *Virtues: For Another Possible World*, 128.
28. Boff, *Virtues: For Another Possible World*, 128.

make the other into his neighbor."²⁹ According to Boff, showing kindness and compassion should not be limited to a specific person. Rather, we should treat everyone with care and understanding, regardless of who they are.

Caring for others means standing by them and working toward alleviating their pain. It involves sharing their suffering, as depicted through the Samaritan's actions. Our response to such encounters is crucial. Rather than condemning those who lack compassion or choose not to help, we should willingly offer our *care-full* attention, evident in our attitudes, to help those who are needy and *care-less*. In this sense, and from a caring perspective, every individual in the parable required care—whether it was physical or emotional. Therefore, we all must be educated in the way of care, albeit in different ways.

The tender care for the other must motivate one to move toward others even if it means "healing on a Saturday," as Jesus did (Mark, 3:1–6), emphasizing that a person comes before the Law. Caring for others is a driving force that leads us to reach out to them, even if it requires sacrificing our own time and effort. Jesus' teachings extended beyond the injured man, the onlookers, or the outcast hero who cared for the wounded man. Instead, Jesus reveals how everyone needs and deserves care, inspiring us to embrace our responsibility in caring for one another, telling us to "go and do likewise."

The Good Samaritan parable teaches us the importance of caring for others beyond ourselves and doing what is right. It highlights that doing what is right may not always mean doing good. Jesus shifts the focus from the person to the action, highlighting that what the Samaritan did was good. Perhaps for him doing the right thing would be avoiding contact with the wounded Jew because of the animosities between the two cultures. Despite the animosity, the Samaritan chose to help the wounded Jew. This illustrates the importance of identifying those needing our care, regardless of nationality, social status, or religion. It serves as a reminder of the value of life. Furthermore, the parable encourages us to consider care not just as an individual responsibility but as a social responsibility in which we all must participate, regardless of our titles, attributions, or duties. Divine intervention is at work to uplift those experiencing hardship and pain. The sentiment of compassion is deeply ingrained in the principles of care, inspiring impactful actions that bring about positive change.

---

29. Boff. *Virtues: For Another Possible World*, 129.

From Care-Less Education to Care-Full Education

The word "pedagogy" has its roots in the Greek words *pais* or *paidos* (meaning "boy" or "child") and *agogus* (meaning "leader" or "guide"), which directly translates to "one who shows the way to a child." Among the Greeks and Romans, the *paidagogos* (teacher) was an educated slave tasked with supervising and disciplining the youngster. In the Hellenistic era, the paidagogos's function changed from that of a teacher who corrects students to that of a teacher of life and knowledge who was also in charge of helping children develop their moral character.[30]

Drawing on the etymological meaning of pedagogue as one who accompanies and observes the pupils' activities, care-full education provided by careful and compassionate educators should concentrate on connections that aim to promote the flourishing of all. An example of promoting coexistence on a planetary level through education is incorporating the concept of "walking-with" into the teaching approach. This involves addressing students' intellectual and spiritual needs and encouraging their creative pursuits. An education that is attentive and care-full involves a mutual connection between the educator and the student, resulting in benefits for both parties in their unique ways.

In the African culture of Kongo, the newborn is welcomed into the community as the "living sun," and Kindezi is the art of helping the "living sun" to shine once they are brought into the physical world. Kindezi, as an art-focused not only on nurturing the youth within the community but also on the growth of the Ndezi (the caregiver), is an ongoing process that encompasses attention, responsibility, and delight. According to Fu-Kiau and Lukondo-Wamba, Kindezi is,

> the art of touching, caring for, and protecting the child's life and the environment, *kinzungidila*, in which the child's multidimensional development takes place. The word "Kindezi," a Kikongo language term, stems itself from the root verb *lela*, which means to enjoy taking and giving special care.[31]

In their poignant portrayal of the African socialization process, the authors emphasize the significance of both the elderly and the young in Kongo society. The community values the spiritual, mental, and cultural fortitude of

---

30. Cully and Cully, eds., *Harper's Encyclopedia of Religious Education*, 478. See also Libaneo, *Pedagogia e Pedagogos*, 25–38.

31. Fu-Kiau and Lukondo-Wamba, *Kindezi*, 1.

the elders, who continue to impart ancestral wisdom and contribute to the cultural development of the younger generations. Kindezi's profound message is that nurturing each "living sun" is a sacred obligation that requires collective effort.

Despite the significant progress and technological advancements, machines are still unable to experience emotions, even with the implementation of artificial "intelligence." They cannot feel pain, get involved, be affected by others, or show empathy. In other words, the ability to be emotional is still beyond their reach. We are beings of love and affection, beings of com-*passion* (with passion) and care. Through our bodies, we perceive and understand the world around us. The precariousness of life leads us to question the unjust systems that categorize and dictate that some lives hold greater value than others. Hence, in our increasingly complex world, it is crucial to think critically about the issue of care in democratic societies. For societies to overcome neglect, they must establish just relationships where everyone is treated with dignity and fairness, including those who, as Butler indicates, have been considered ungrievable. To dismantle a culture of carelessness and indifference, it is essential to cultivate attitudes through which it is possible to prioritize the well-being of all individuals by offering them resources, empathy and support.

Care must be incorporated into our answers to the current planetary challenges in light of the interconnectedness of humans and the environment, the ethics of care, social and environmental justice, resilience, and sustainable culture. Exercising care is conceiving a world of loving relationships, harmony, and solidarity among people. When we recognize our need to care and be cared for, we reveal our shared humanity and confront our vulnerabilities and limitations, inspiring us to imagine care otherwise. To promote constructive conversations and positive connections, moving away from a mentality of scarcity and competition is essential. This shift requires a thoughtful approach to education that goes beyond mere reasoning and involves a heartfelt desire to create meaningful connections.

While rational analysis may emphasize measuring outcomes and results, education that genuinely cares is fueled by empathy. It enhances growth and collaboration. This means seeing schools as spaces for cultivating creativity and kindness where individuals can develop and thrive. Therefore, we can establish a more harmonious way of coexisting by embracing compassion, solidarity, and love for ourselves, others, and the planet. Such *care-full* education lays the essential groundwork for a more promising future.

5

Principles to *Sulear* Our Pedagogies

> I seek to undress myself from what I have learned,
> I seek to forget how to remember what was taught,
> And to scratch the ink with which my senses were painted,
> Unpack my true emotions, unload myself and be me . . .
> The essential is to know how to see.
> But this (sad for us who bring the soul clothed) requires a profound study,
> An apprenticeship in unlearning . . .
>
> —Fernando Pessoa

Rubem Alves, Brazilian theologian, educator, and poet, in his book *Conversas com Quem Gosta de Ensinar* (Conversations with Those Who Like to Teach), offers an insightful analogy to distinguish between teachers and educators. He believes that teachers are defined by their external appearance and performance, while educators are defined by their innermost being, by the heart, and by vocation. He says,

> Teachers are comparable to old trees, with unique faces, names, and stories to tell. They exist in a world where the bond they share with each student is what matters most. Each student, being a *sui generis* entity, bearer of a name, also of a story, he or she suffers sadness and nurtures hope. Education happens in this invisible

Principles to *Sulear* Our Pedagogies

but intricate space created by the teacher-student relationship. Indeed, an artisanal space.[1]

Although sycamore[2] and eucalyptus trees are made of the same essence—wood—they are not the same. They each have their habitat and location in the world of trees. According to Alves, sycamores belong to the world of mystery and thrive and grow old in their habitat. Eucalyptus trees, conversely, grow rapidly and abundantly, making them easy to cultivate and from which profit is more easily generated. Unlike ancient trees that no human may have witnessed grow from seed to grandiose tree, eucalyptus trees can be easily replaced if necessary. Alves suggests,

> "For some people, eucalyptus trees are more beautiful because they grow all lined up, in a permanent sentinel position, prepared for cutting. However, for this reason, eucalyptus does not have stories to tell, secrets to keep, revelations to disclose, or mysteries to share like the ancient trees."[3]

Alves argues that vocations and professions are like trees. They grow in ecological niches according to circumstances that impel them to come to existence. Still, when outside their habitat, they grow weaker, deteriorate, and eventually may disappear. Alves states that educators are like old trees. They have a countenance, a name, a story to tell. They live in a world in which what counts is the relationship they establish with the students, who also possess a name and a story to share. In his mind, educators inhabit a world in which people are defined by their visions, passions, hopes, and utopic horizons. I agree with Alves that visions, hope, and imagination drive educators, the latter being, as Maxime Greene puts it, "the means by which we can build a coherent world that makes empathy possible"[4] and, in doing so, we "release our imagination."

Throughout the preceding chapters, I have put forth the idea that a pedagogy for planetary *convivência* requires certain qualities, including a mindful acknowledgment of our planetary existence and empathetic attitudes that enable us to coexist peacefully with humans and more-than-humans. These qualities align with the traits of educators, as described by

---

1. Alves, *Conversas com Quem Gosta de Ensinar,* 13.

2. In this book, Alves refers to the Jequitibá tree, which I translated as Sycamore (Platanus occidentalis) because it is the closest tree regarding its height and appearance.

3. Alves, *Conversas,* 12 (free translation).

4. Greene, *Releasing the Imagination,* 3.

Alves. Therefore, just like old trees that spread their roots deeply in search of nutrients, we also need to delve deeper into our understanding of what it means to participate and collaborate with constructing a world of justice for all. We must resist the temptation of quick fixes and superficial responses that only offer the illusion of solving our complex and immeasurable problems. When we focus only on the tools in our toolbox, on the performative inclinations, or the compartmentalization of knowledge, we limit our ability to see beyond people's names and be attentive to people's stories and wisdom.

As we move beyond our toolbox, it becomes possible to comprehend the emotional needs of our students. We recognize their yearning for a sense of belonging and remain mindful of the traumas they may have experienced. Furthermore, we might delve deep within ourselves to identify our own yearnings and traumas. In our journey toward a more authentic way of seeing and being, we must develop what Parker Palmer calls "soft eyes," inspired by Japanese self-defense techniques. According to Palmer, by cultivating soft eyes we allow ourselves to expand our peripheral vision and better perceive our surroundings.[5] In his description, soft eyes are a learned skill through which we broaden our vision to take in "the grandeur of the world and the grace of great things." From the perspective of the pedagogy for planetary *convivência*, not only do we need soft eyes, but soft words and gentle gestures through which we can awaken our sensitivity to perceive the pain and suffering of all created things.

As old trees, when deeply rooted, we can withstand challenges and access the nutrients we need to stay resilient. So that when life's challenges, emotional outbursts, and historical ruptures arise, impacting human civilizing processes, we can face them with resilience and hope. These moments, characterized by interruptions, cracks, suspensions, symbolic and material discontinuities, or breaches in our way of organizing ourselves as a society, can work in our favor. When disruptions shake up our lives, they bring with them new perspectives and opportunities. These unexpected events give us the chance to redirect our thinking and actions, paving the way for growth. Paradigmatic changes are the result of profound ruptures that prompt us to reorganize life. Among the many characteristics that mark these fissures, we can name at least two of them: a deep pain for the "death" of the known, the familiar, of what we have loved, valued, and knew, and a momentary blockage evidenced by a disconcerting sensation that the

---

5. Palmer, *The Courage to Teach*, 113.

Principles to *Sulear* Our Pedagogies

unknown provokes. During these times of expectation, uncertainties, and the pain of shattered dreams, we inhabit a chaotic yet creative liminal space full of potential.

As a planetary community, we have endured many times of rupture and chaos. Although it seems unusual, some of us find solace in knowing that, even from afar, we are all embarking on a collective journey with thousands of people from all corners of the earth. Some of us, however, have discovered how difficult it is to live with what and who we have become. During periods of uncertainty, we find the need to create routines and invent new ways of living with ourselves and others. We realize that we must improvise new rituals of lament, mourning, and contemplation. For instance, during the coronavirus pandemic, we realized that a new spirituality would be necessary to survive such turbulent times. The pandemic has had a profound impact on the lives of many, and it's important to acknowledge that some people have lost certain privileges, comforts, and freedoms that they once enjoyed. Upon closer examination, we can see that there are certain communities—such as Black, indigenous, riverside communities, immigrants, and impoverished populations—that are already battling pandemics in their daily lives. These pandemics, often go unnoticed by many, take many forms, including hunger, racism, violence, exclusion, and mass death. These "made vulnerable" populations were not only the most affected by the pandemic but also revealed the most perverse side of the current socioeconomic/geopolitical system and its cruel and unfair face of planetary calamity.

In this theater of cruelty, leaders' neglect, misinformation, and omissions generated an actual genocide against indigenous, Blacks, and inhabitants of poorer regions, proliferating the precarity of life in devastating ways. During the pandemic, we experienced a significant shift in our world, leading us to reevaluate the extravagant activities that once defined a globalized world. In these trying times, we faced the need to reconsider our values and priorities. Thus, when the light stage of such "liquid life"[6] went out, imposing on us physical distancing, we were obliged to turn our attention to our inner world. We were forced to look at ourselves to discover what remained of our humanity. We had to collect our thoughts, sensitivities, and identities, gather our feelings, align our bodies, sensations, and affections, re-cadence our rhythms, examine our connections, face our frustrations, re-direct our desires, re-think even what a priority in the face

---

6. Bauman, *Modernidade Líquida*, 2001.

of a pandemic emergency would be. In this introspective exercise of travel to the center of ourselves and a retrospective exercise of revisiting our past, we sought out the elements that could feed, sustain, and comfort us during this time of recollection.

In that time of injunction, to use a term adopted by cultural anthropologist Victor Turner, we were separated from the usual course of our routines and the social groups to which we belonged and interacted with. We began to live an experience on the margins of the social structure and the references that identified us and by which we guided our lives.[7] We have not yet reached the third phase, called re-aggregation identified by Turner.[8] We are, however, in the border zone, in the interstitial moment between how we have perceived the world and lived our lives before the pandemic and how we are navigating this post-pandemic world that signals the eminence of another pandemic on the horizon. We do not know for sure what to expect. Still, we know that we need to think of this frontier time as a time of gestation of the new through which we can recover what is left of our suffocated humanity, imagining it as a time to cultivate our resistance, sharpening our ability to discern reality, awakening our sensitivity to the suffering of everyone, and thus collectively weaving a new form of *convivência* based on mutuality, reciprocity, and affection.

For Turner, the concept of liminality constitutes a transitional period, a process, a becoming. It is a transformation period in which culture, individual perception, and reality are confronted, examined, and practiced through rituals. He states that liminality is the intermediate time-space in which cultural values are incorporated, and new situations can be experienced paradoxically. In the injunction, it is possible to experience highly creative, ambiguous, marginal, transgressive, and transformative conditions. Turner believes that liminal experience has the potential to transform or subvert dominant social structures by offering alternative paradigms of how society could be conceived through social dramas.[9]

Thinking about challenging and disruptive moments from a liminal perspective means embracing their disorientation and potentiality. It

---

7. In his book, *The Ritual Process*, building on van Gennep's concept of rites of passage, Turner demonstrated that there are three distinct phases in all well-structured (constructed) rituals: separation, liminality, and re-aggregation. He argues that usually, during the threshold phase or liminal state, people can experience themselves and their reality from a new point of view.

8. Turner, *The Ritual Process*, 94–130.

9. Turner, *The Ritual Process*, 94–95.

means admitting that the challenges experienced could be fruitful to the extent that new ideas and forms of coexistence could emerge. In this borderline space, even if unable to alleviate the pains and anxieties that surface from our hearts, we feel the pulse of life that, even shy, runs through our arteries and circulates through our bodies as an invisible force—a germ (virus) of resilience and transformation—animating us not to give up on life. We can view the perplexing situation as an opportunity to learn and gain knowledge. A favorable moment to adjust our approach to education and consider new ways to address the challenges. This, indeed, will guide us along ecologically and humanly defensible paths. Challenging times reveal the human capacity to seek alternatives to redesign life and to observe how societies can adapt to new ways of life when necessary and urgent. Thus, we have a propitious moment to think about options for how we live our lives and relate to one another. And just as we adjust our lives to those situations, we can also invent new ways to resist, challenge our epistemologies, correct our pedagogies, and create new forms of coexistence. This hope encourages me to imagine what principles would help us in this journey of the unknown.

One of Freire's most famous premises concerns the educability of human beings, which implies that we are not finished beings, but beings in the process of transformation. I consider Freire's notion of becoming comprehensive because it is continuous—a process that should not be fragmented. Whenever one begins uncritically to accept a model that fragments humans to the point of boxing them in, something more fundamental to our humanity is lost: human agency. Freire's notion of becoming is central to what it means to become fully human. We become human as we construct history with others through culture, language, and the creation and use of instruments and signs. The history we build with other human beings is part of a continuous process of development that includes intellectual, ethical, social, and transcendental components.

In our path of becoming, through our experiences, activities, and everyday interactions, we are doers, contemplators, producers of knowledge, dreamers, transformers, and beings of memories and affection. As members of a culture that provides us tools for organizing and understanding our world, we embark on an adventurous quest to construct meanings that bring happiness and a sense of purpose to our lives. Not only do we search for meaning, but also, we are beings capable of giving meaning to our existence. Therefore, we are human beings who not only live but exist.

A Pedagogy for Planetary *Convivência*

According to Freire,[10] to exist means more than to be in the world, it means to be with the world. This understanding incorporates the vital aptitudes we need to transcend, discern, dialogue, and participate in our culture as social and cultural agents. Even though we start from ourselves, our interaction with others shapes these critical abilities. Nita Freire affirms that for Freire, "Existence is deeply marked by an ethical-political-educational concern of human beings. It is a human experience that opens possibilities for men and women to speak expressing their most elaborate thoughts and their most genuine emotions."[11] Existence is intrinsically linked to dreams, to the utopia of a better and more just world, and when, for whatever reason, the dreams are interrupted, human beings are prevented from existing in their fullness.

In our daily lives, we face challenges like racism, injustice, competition, consumerism, and individualism that seek to stifle, block, and diminish our life experiences. However, we also have at our reach intrinsic abilities to overcome these impediments as we continue to search for the welfare of every being, both human and more than human. The desire to pursue another form of existence on this planet does not come naturally or effortlessly—reaching a state of wholeness where all things are integrated and dependable—but needs to be educated. As unfinished beings within a historical yet unfinished human condition, we realize that our incompleteness allows us to improve ourselves, overcome obstacles, and discover new paths toward human expansiveness.

Studies and discoveries in neuroscience have examined and analyzed the plasticity and ability of the human mind to adapt and reinvent itself in the face of life's obstacles. However, the human intelligence that invented extraordinary artifacts and significantly advanced knowledge about all aspects of life also perfected the tools of destruction. Thus, instead of promoting the means to improve life on Earth, this advance has led to the deterioration of human living conditions and environmental tragedies, accelerating global warming and, thus, putting life at significant risk. In a way, scientific and technological development in recent decades has made human life and the life of other species on the planet practically unviable. In light of this reality, it is essential to emphasize that technology should never replace human agency, no matter how advanced it may be. That is why we need to problematize how profit-maximizing technology can potentially

---

10. Freire, *Educação como Prática da Liberdade*, 57.
11. Freire (Nita) org, *Pedagogia dos Sonhos Possíveis*, 15–16.

eliminate human agency and exacerbate the already unpleasant inequality between countries of the North and South. Planetary destruction and the risk of discontinuity of life on Earth have never been so plausible or so close. In the eloquent words of Martin Luther King, Jr., spoken many decades ago,

> When we look at modern man [sic] we have to face the fact that modern man [sic] suffers from a kind of poverty of the spirit, which stands in glaring contrast to his scientific and technological abundance. We've learned to fly the air like birds, we've learned to swim the seas like fish, and yet we haven't learned to walk the earth as brothers and sisters.[12]

Regrettably, his utterance remains relevant in the current context characterized by rapid socio-political-economic change, ever-expanding global interconnection, and the deterioration of human relations. Instead of learning how to live with one another, we have witnessed what Henry Giroux[13] brilliantly calls a "culture of cruelty" and a "politics of humiliation" through which a set of values, policies, and symbolic practices legitimize forms of organized violence against bodies, predominantly black and brown bodies. Such cruelty practiced in various spheres of society has become part of the social fabric rehearsed through a pedagogy of cruelty as defined by Argentine sociologist, Rita Sagato:

> When I speak of a pedagogy of cruelty, I am referring to something very precise, such as the capture of something that flowed errantly and unpredictably, such as life, to install there the inertia and sterility of the thing, measurable, profitable, buyable, and obsolescent, as is appropriate for consumption in this apocalyptic phase of capital. (. . .) The repetition of violence produces a normalizing effect on a landscape of cruelty and, with this, promotes in people the low thresholds of empathy essential for the predatory enterprise. Habitual cruelty is directly proportional to forms of narcissistic and consumerist enjoyment and to the isolation of citizens through their desensitization to the suffering of others.[14]

The culture that has promoted a normalization of cruelty perpetrated against marginalized individuals and groups has also been practiced against

---

12. Eyewitness News report from February 27, 1967, in San Francisco, featuring scenes from a sermon by Rev. Dr. Martin Luther King, Jr.
13. Giroux. *Education and Crisis of Public Values*, 15.
14. Segato, *Contra-pedagogías de la crueldad*, 11.

our planet. Examining our lifestyle, we can see that we still haven't learned to relate and live harmoniously with those who think and are different from us. We have not learned to eradicate multiple racism and racialized formations within the places we belong and within ourselves, and even less so in contexts where demographic shifts, displacement, immigration flows, genocides, ecocides, femicides, and new forms of colonialism have grown exponentially.

The harshness of capitalism is taking a toll on our ecosystem. Unfortunately, we have not yet fully grasped the significance of establishing a relationship with the environment that is less exploitative and less destructive. The environment is a space that houses all forms of life and, therefore, deserves to be treated with care and respect. Capitalism is an economic system that places great importance on maximizing profits. In many cases, this means that the interests of people and resources can be overlooked or even excluded. The drive for profit can lead to the exploitation of resources, often creating environmental damage and depletion of natural resources. Additionally, the focus on profit can result in the exclusion of certain groups of people from economic opportunities, particularly those who are marginalized or living in poverty. Ultimately, the pursuit of profits can lead to a concentration of wealth and power among a few, while leaving many others behind.

As a planetary community, we have witnessed unprecedented natural disasters and resource shortages, which have impacted life in general and impoverished some communities more drastically than others. These underprivileged communities are doomed to a life—or non-life—that lacks the essentials necessary to live, eat, work, have access to education and housing, and many other aspects that constitute a life lived with dignity. These communities, situated in remote regions of the world and on the outskirts of developed metropolises, face many challenges.

Our planet, too, is agonizing. Our forests have been severely damaged, several species of animals are on the brink of extinction. In some regions, our water supply is scarce or restricted. The planet is ill, and its lungs are already showing indications of weakening. Its convulsed rivers are disturbed and bursting with despair, and its forests are aflame with fever. The turmoil of a world in a rush that cannot stop causes the earth to groan in muted screams to the sound of factories, horns, human agglomerations, and land devastation. Natural resources have had less time to rebuild themselves because of the acceleration of such a path of destruction. Little has been done to avert this calamity despite the recommendations of scientists and environmentalists, and our outlook on life continues to be "business as usual." Even the latest calamities have not been able significantly to alter a society's rhythm that, after a momentary pause in activity, quickly resumed its self-delusional return to "normality." Because a world driven by the metrics of capitalism and neoliberal principles prefers to remain "in the pandemic fog of social and historical amnesia," as Henry Giroux reminds us.[15]

As the earth suffers and struggles, humans are also deteriorating and losing their connection to themselves, others, and the world around them. In our rush to get somewhere without knowing where or why, we're distancing ourselves from the land that sustains us. We've become strangers to the place we call home. By forgetting our cosmic home, we're losing ourselves. Our economic logic, based on the idea of extractivism, hides the loss of essential elements that sustain life on the planet, causing harm to all living beings. However, what seems to be a path of no return can be redone, repaired, and recovered *when* and *if* there is at least the will to learn to reconnect with what is our essence, as well as the commitment to adopt ecologically viable economic systems and to prioritize an emancipatory education. Though difficult, we can slow down the frenetic pace of our lives and build our lives on different foundations. We can re-educate ourselves to rebuild new horizons of justice for all, to relearn how to be with others, to take care of one another, to inhabit our homeland, and to change our consumption habits. Sometimes, when we are coerced to stop the frantic pace of our lives due to circumstances and forces beyond our control, we realize that there are more important things to achieve than being consumed by the frenetic pace of life. Challenging situations often help us gain a deeper understanding of what is truly important in our lives. After such experiences, we can take the opportunity to re-focus our priorities and make necessary changes that align better with our values and purposes.

The Rivers That Cross Us[16]

As I wonder how to construct the premises of a pedagogy for planetary *convivência*, as one pathway among others, I recall the wisdom of the rivers

---

15. Giroux, *Race, Politics, and Pandemic Pedagogy*, xiii.

16. I recently had the honor of participating in a conference on environmental education in the Brazilian Amazon region. During the flight, I was dazzled by the rivers that flow sinuously throughout the state of Pará. A breathtaking moment that left a deep

as Ailton Krenak, Brazilian writer, journalist, philosopher, activist, and indigenous movement leader of Krenak ethnicity, mentions in his book *Futuro Ancestral* (Ancestral Future).[17] In this book, small in size but large in wisdom, the author says that rivers are beings that have always inhabited the world in different ways. He observes that rivers change course when they face obstacles. In 2015, when a dam belonging to a multinational mining company broke, destroying the life that existed in the *Rio Doce* almost its entire length, some people said that the river was dead. To this day, the waters remain muddy and polluted with mining waste and heavy metals, and the fish that still survive there are not fit for consumption, and no one can drink its water. Krenak believes the river is not dead but in a *coma state* and will eventually change its course in the face of this man-make tragedy. He trusts that *Rio Doce* will find new subterranean paths to move forward and reach its destiny, the ocean. Krenak advises us: "Let us be water, in matter and spirit, in our movement and ability to change course, or we will be lost."[18]

Rivers are fundamental for human survival. Rivers are important in everyday life and, more specifically, to the lives of those who inhabit their banks. They represent a source of energy and knowledge. I concur with Krenak that rivers are more than water; they are beings with history and resilience. In the artwork of Earth's natural wonders, rivers, with their sinuous paths and fluid grace, hold a profound significance for human survival and delight. They are the lifeblood of our planet, nourishing the world and enchanting our senses. Rivers flow like veins, connecting distant realms and carrying life's essence within them. They are the conduits through which water, the elixir of existence, reaches our fields and farms, quenching the thirst for crops and sustaining the livelihood of those who toil with hope and resilience. They sculpt the land with patient grace, carving deep canyons and meandering valleys that witness their timeless journey. As they travel, rivers offer respite and enchantment to those who seek solace in their embrace. But the significance of rivers extends far beyond their aesthetic charm. They are the lifelines connecting civilizations and cultures, flowing through bustling cities and quiet towns. Throughout history, rivers have served as conduits for trade and communication, bearing the dreams and stories of countless generations. They have witnessed the rise and fall of

---

impression on me.

17. Krenak, *Futuro Ancestral*.
18. Krenak, *Futuro Ancestral*, 27.

ancient civilizations and seen the ebb and flow of human endeavors. They are the arteries of thriving metropolises, supplying water for industries, nourishing communities, and enabling the harmonious coexistence of humans and nature. Rivers offer a sense of connectivity, a tangible reminder that we are all interconnected by the flow of life.

Rivers have always marked the history of my family. My paternal grandmother lived very close to a river, and during the rainy season, when the water level surpassed the bed, it flooded the entire area. During that period, people had to leave their homes until the rivers settled down and returned to their ordinary course. My grandmother had to learn when to remain and when it was time to leave her home. She needed to learn to read the movements of the river and to adapt to its oscillations and its flux. She needed to learn how to dance respectfully with nature and not try to dominate what is natural and, sometimes, beyond our control.

My maternal grandmother was an interesting woman who taught herself to read by begging for access to the books of her brothers; when later in life, she became the mother of four girls and a boy, she instilled in them the importance of studying and always encouraged them to learn how to read and write. They lived in a remote town surrounded by rivers. The rivers were decisive in my mother's and her siblings' education. During the months of heavy rain in the region, the river spread out and took part of the road that would take them to school. During those months, it was impossible to cross the river. Hence, they had to continue the schooling at home, creating a process that Freire would later call untested feasibility (*inédito viável*).

For many people in different regions of the planet, rivers cross and radically modify the daily lives of many families. As it was in my mother's case, the rivers *sulearam* the educational processes in her family and marked a season in the life of my aunties and uncle. In a way, the rivers pushed my grandparents, my parents, and their siblings to imagine new cartographies despite the impossibility of "moving forward." Confronting adversities, instead of retreating, they embarked on this crossing and joined together to give vent to the flow of life with creativity, responsibility, and respect for nature. I would say that, somehow, they understood what the rivers were trying to tell them and could stop what they were doing to allow the power of the rivers to flow naturally. Moreover, they become rivers themselves carving new pathways to overcome the limit-situations.

A Pedagogy for Planetary *Convivência*

Each of us has stories that shape our memories and invite us to think about our wanderings in facing the struggles, uncertainties, and changes in life. In our crossings, many people, circumstances, and movements provide elements to help us in our journey. Even when we are too busy to pay attention to the movement of everything in our pathway, they provide us with their wisdom. The great lesson my grandmothers left me was to retrace the paths of the waters, internal and external, that are always in motion before me, sometimes turbulent, sometimes calmer. In this coming and going of the water movement, I ask myself to which movements I have been letting my body sway. In what waters do I let myself bathe? Do I allow the delicate balance that sustains them and ensures their health and vitality to endure for future generations? Do I let them teach me how to live my life? In the rivers' embrace we find our survival and our delight. They awaken our senses, inspire admiration, and alert us to the need to preserve them, as they are a source of life and well-being for countless species that depend on them. They invite us to reflect on the wonders of creation and our place in it, for in the rhythmic flow of rivers, we discover the interconnectedness of all living things and the timeless wonder that accompanies life's journey.

As human beings, we are marked and shaped as people by the contexts and social places we inhabit, by the experiences we live, by the social roles we occupy, and by the relationships we establish, be they power, submission, or mutuality, including the appreciation we have for the world that surrounds us. That is, the culture that humans create with nature is designed to enhance the *buen vivir* in harmony with the gifts we were bestowed—gifts that make life treasured without the need to commodify it so as to expand inequality gaps. While acknowledging these connections, I like to think that it's not the places we inhabit that define us but **how** we relate to the humans and non-humans around us and **how** we position ourselves in the interstices of the cultural fabric, despite attempts to define ourselves according to standards alien to our desires, our dreams, our territories. For this reason, it is fundamental for me to be attentive to the maps we create in our narratives and the paths they lead us on.

As a critical educator, my proposal in this writing is to give rise to reflection on the ways in which we have been relating to each other in our pedagogical interactions that extend beyond the walls of schools. In our diverse and chaotic contexts of inequality, violence, and scarcity, we need to resist the forces that seek to separate us from ourselves and the people we love. The utopian dimension of education is an attempt to demonstrate that the freedom to think, create, live, and wonder is not possible as a prefabricated educational model, but as an expansive and generous pulsation that affirms through our concrete actions that the world can be transformed. Imagining this world is a call to embrace the lives of children, women, people of color, indigenous peoples, immigrants, and all those who are under siege every day and everywhere. In our collective effort to imagine another kind of world for our sons and daughters, we need to reflect on how we will position ourselves and protect the lives of those who are vulnerabilized, meaning the ongoing process through which vulnerability is created and sustained in our societies. How are we going to break these cycles of violence, stop the suffering, heal the trauma, and prevent the angel of death from spreading through our schools and communities?

In my modest effort, I imagine that a possible answer is to rescue the connection of mind and heart that bring us back to our humanity and to release the feelings that the traditional school tries to suppress, block, devalue. To achieve a viable pedagogy for planetary *convivência*, we must let ourselves be guided by the bonds of affectivity and delicate threads of tenderness, letting them weave human relationships. I'm not advocating corny feelings to help us to forget the ugliness of a world immersed in cruelty. I'm speaking of feelings cultivated from a critical consciousness that recognizes why they should be part of our pedagogical interactions. The principles that I deem vital for an emancipatory pedagogical practice constitute an alternative to the references proposed by Western thought. They seek to inspire other types of realities to be built not for the purposes of "development and progress" but for the purpose of involvement, commitment, and embrace of people as they seek to live their full potential. That's why I am calling them principles to *sulear* our pedagogies inspired by the work of Paulo Freire.

Freire's liberation pedagogy has had a lasting impact on education through his innovative ideas and transformative approach. Central to his educational philosophy are concepts such as hope, love, dialogue, and solidarity, among many others. In the sequence of this chapter, I will explore the significance of these concepts, their relevance to the planetary pedagogy for *convivência*, and how they inspire us to engage critically with planetary challenges as we envision a more equitable and sustainable world. I will begin by introducing the term *sulear* used by Freire, which I believe is essential to conceptualize this pedagogy.

A Pedagogy for Planetary *Convivência*

Freirean Principles to *Sulear* Our Pedagogies

The word *sulear* was used by Freire in his book *Pedagogia da Esperança* (*Pedagogy of Hope*, 1996), as he revisited his pedagogical praxis initiated in the early 1960s. Ana Maria Araujo Freire, in her explanatory notes in this book, provides historical context to Freire's radical thought, helping readers understand the conditions and pressures under which he wrote his books. She also stressed that Márcio Campos was the intellectual who called Freire's attention to the ideology implicit in the term. She discusses Freire's interpretation of the term *sulear* in her Note 15, saying,

> Paulo Freire has used the term *sulear-se*—which does not actually exist in dictionaries of the Portuguese language—to call readers' attention to the ideological connotation of the terms *orientar-se*, to "orientate oneself" (lit., point oneself to the east, get one's bearings from the east), *orientação* (orientation)," *nortear-se* (a synonym for *orientar-se*, but in terms of the north rather than the east), and suchlike derivatives of the Portuguese words for 'east' and 'north.'"[19]

The Portuguese term *nortear* translates to "orient or guide" in English, indicating that its meaning is intimately connected to the understanding that what directs or leads an individual comes from the north or the north is the direction to move forward. This concept is deeply rooted in Brazilian culture, so much that the word to describe a person without direction is *des-norteada*, meaning "a person without north." According to Nita Freire, Freire's choice to use the term *sulear* is to highlight that we, people of the South, should not ignore our ability to construct knowledge that incorporates our struggles, desires, and potentialities for breaking free from alienation and the colonization of our minds and bodies.

For a long time, the hegemonic process of perpetuating Eurocentric values and epistemologies hindered the recovery of indigenous knowledge that Freire talks about. This prevented the development of epistemologies that could reflect, question, and add knowledge to expand thoughts and perspectives on education and educational practices. Freire stands out as a timeless intellectual who recognizes these manipulations of Eurocentric perspectives, rejecting the idea of an instrumental results-driven banking education and instead advocating for a liberating approach.

---

19. Ana Maria Araújo Freire, Notes 15, in Freire, *Pedagogy of Hope*, 192.

Principles to *Sulear* Our Pedagogies

Freire declares that dehumanization—a concrete historical fact—is not a destiny but manufactured by the unjust order that generates violence and exclusion. His pedagogical insights show an evident commitment to the struggles of subaltern groups and their effort to develop a counter-hegemonic perspective that would break with colonial domination. For him, if, on the one hand, colonialism acted as an obstacle to the democratic project, education should awaken the people's consciousness to understand their reality. Thus, education in a democratic society becomes "education as a practice of freedom." His ethical responsibility toward the "wretched of the earth," with those denied their place in the cosmos, as well as his repudiation of prejudices and sinister acts committed against any human being, has always been highlighted in his books and his encounters with people worldwide. In his book, *Education as the Practice of Freedom*,[20] he declares that a non-alienating educational effort would become a crucial element in guiding society through a process of decolonization, progressively shedding the chains of its colonial past.

From his first writings, Freire denounced the influence of colonialism in all forms and defended the value of popular cultures, their memories, their ancestry, and wisdom. He established a permanent and constructive dialogue with them throughout the educational process, developing work strategies that would enable the oppressed to uncover their oppression, and, as a result, they would work toward transforming their limiting conditions. Freire's ethical sensitivity not only made him sensitive to the suffering of others but impelled him to respect the ancestral knowledge of these populations, encouraging them to develop their critical capacity and resilience to fight against injustices and collectively build a world where it would be easier to love. As Enrique Dussel, Argentine-Mexican philosopher, historian and theologian, states in his book *Ethics of Liberation in the Age of Globalization and Exclusion,* "Freire is not just an educator in the strict sense of the term. He is something more—an educator of the "ethical-critical conscience" of the victims, the oppressed, the condemned of the planet who live in community.[21]

Drawing from Freire's significant contributions to education, particularly his insightful proposal of generative themes, I suggest a similar approach to lay the groundwork for pedagogy for planetary *convivência*. Out of the numerous concepts he developed throughout his life, I have chosen

---

20. Freire, *Education as the Practice of Freedom*, 35.
21. Dussel, *Ethics of Liberation*, 303.

A Pedagogy for Planetary *Convivência*

Hope, Lovingness, Dialogue, and Solidarity as generative words that can form a positive and constructive basis for the envisioned pedagogy.

As Freire eloquently posits, generative themes, underpinned by generative words, are not stagnant or fixed but overflowing with potential meanings. They are dynamic and evolving, serving as creative and imaginative spaces that ignite our epistemological curiosity. These themes, born from our daily encounters, culminate in syntheses about our sociocultural reality. Generative words, inseparable from life's struggles, relationships, or knowledge, are part of a dynamic process open to modifications and expansions. Their creative potential and contextual relevance keep them in a constant state of evolution. This dynamism stimulates both the mind and emotions, keeping us engaged and intrigued.

The principles outlined here are not recipes to be followed. They point to reassessing the complex sociocultural and political reality in which we are involved. Moreover, they aim to encourage the convergence of ideas through dialogue and thus provide a more comprehensive grasp of our reality, the place we occupy, and what changes we can generate.

The Power of Hope in Freire's Pedagogy

Hope is a vital principle in Freire's pedagogy, serving as a catalyst for societal transformation and human liberation. Freire's work with oppressed communities influenced his conviction in the transformational power of hope. In *Pedagogy of Hope*, he underscores the importance of hope as a motivator for action and empowerment stating, "I do not understand human existence, and the struggle needed to improve it, apart from hope."[22] Instead of becoming paralyzed by personal and worldwide adverse events, Freire reminds us that these occurrences should not lead us into despair but rather inspire us to fight with hope against fatalism and inaction. Likewise, he insists that the emblematic dehumanization of our contexts is not a reason for despair but for the hope that leads us to the incessant search for the humanization of all in solidarity with those made invisible in our societies. Freire says education is a potent tool for creating critical consciousness and cultivating hope. An education as the practice of freedom, becomes the "means by which men and women deal critically and creatively with reality and discover how to participate in the transformation of their world."[23] For

---

22. Freire, *Pedagogy of Hope*, 2
23. Freire, *Pedagogy of the Oppressed*, 16.

this reason, he believes that the conventional banking model of education, in which information is transmitted to passive students, does not work, and defends instead a liberating education.

The Need to Educate Our Hope

According to Freire, hope is not a mere wishful thinking but an active and critical stance that prompts individuals to envision a better future and encourages them to take concrete steps toward its realization by relying on their agency in their becoming. So, hope "as an ontological necessity, demands an anchoring in practice."[24] As a necessary aspect of existence, ontological necessity, hope requires practical application to manifest as a tangible reality in history. Thus, while recognizing the importance of hope, grounded in real-world action to become a concrete historical force, Freire admits that hope alone is not enough, which leads him to recognize "the need for a kind of education in hope."[25] Hope, as a vital axis to guide and sustain the renewal of the educational task, requires recognizing that as unfinished beings, we must learn to face challenging situations with hope. Freire states,

> The matrix of hope is the same as the educability of the human being: the incompleteness of his being of which he became conscious. It would be an aggressive contradiction if, unfinished and conscious of the incompleteness, the human being did not enter into a permanent process of hopeful search. (. . .) we have never, perhaps, had more need to emphasize, in educational practice, the sense of hope than today.[26]

Thus, when educated, hope can produce a particular conviction that overcoming a circumstantial necessity is possible, which, in turn, should lead to a series of actions that will contribute to changing unwanted realities. In this context, the role of critical educators becomes fundamental. Freire affirms,

> One of the tasks of the progressive educator, through a serious, correct political analysis, is to unveil opportunities for hope, no matter what obstacles may be. After all, without hope there is little we can do. It will be hard to struggle on, and when we fight as

---

24. Freire, *Pedagogy of Hope*, 2.
25. Freire, *Pedagogy of Hope*, 3.
26. Freire, *Pedagogy of Indignation*, 100.

hopeless or despairing persons, our struggle is suicidal. We shall be beside ourselves, drop our weapons, and throw ourselves into sheer hand-to-hand, purely vindictive, combat.[27]

In his educational approach, Freire not only draws attention to the dimension of human educability in hope and to the role of critical educators in this endeavor, but he extends the notion of hope to encompass a commitment to social justice and the transformation of society.

Hope: A Necessary Ethical Requirement

In *Pedagogy of Freedom,* he writes, "It is impossible to humanly exist without assuming the right and duty to opt, to decide, to struggle, to be political...which in its turn lead us to the radical hope."[28] Thus, to hope means to struggle. Freire's pedagogy of hope carries an ethical imperative that transcends individual aspirations and extends to collective responsibility. To unlock the potential of genuine hope, we must all work together to prioritize justice, fairness, and the overall welfare of all living beings on Earth. Educators who embrace Freire's pedagogy of hope recognize its role in shaping socially conscious and ethically responsible global citizens.

The pedagogy for planetary *convivência* echoes this ethical imperative, emphasizing the importance of recognizing the interdependence of all living things and the need to work together to address local and global issues. It recognizes that it is impossible to educate people in isolation from events happening elsewhere and affecting people locally. The vision of hope as a force that transcends individualism and inspires collective action aligns with the objectives of the pedagogy for planetary *convivência*, which aim to instill a sense of responsibility and ethical care for the planet and its inhabitants. Therefore, such pedagogy recognizes with Freire that a potential *convivência* inevitably begins with the recognition of the presence and value of others. He states: "I like to be a person precisely because of my ethical and political responsibility before the world and other people. I cannot be if others are not; above all, I cannot be if I forbid others from being."[29] Within the context of this conceivable pedagogy, this critical hope, rooted in an understanding of the interconnectedness of social and ecological

---

27. Freire, *Pedagogy of Hope*, 3.
28. Freire, *Pedagogy of Freedom*, 53.
29. Freire, *Pedagogy of the Heart*, 59.

systems, serves as a catalyst for transformational change of our minds and hearts. It is an approach that seeks to promote a sense of interconnectivity, social responsibility, and environmental stewardship, which resonates with Freire's concept of hope. Hope acts as a bridge between comprehending the complexity of global challenges and taking significant action to address them in its framework of the pedagogy of *convivência*. By encouraging students to get involved in their communities, advocate for causes they believe in, or take part in sustainability projects, educators can help students transform their hope into purposeful action. Furthermore, the pedagogy of hope encourages students to consider themselves active participants in promoting change, which aligns with the need for planetary education that cultivates environmentally and socially conscious citizens.

Freire's contributions to education, particularly his emphasis on hope, offer a strong foundation for fostering planetary consciousness and anticipating social change. The goals of the pedagogy I am advocating perfectly align with Freire's pedagogy of hope, which gives students the skills to engage critically with complicated global issues. In this regard, hope is closely intertwined with the concept of conscientization.[30] Through discussions and critical thinking, learners understand the systemic inequalities that contribute to global crises and analyze the root causes of these issues. By encouraging critical consciousness, ethical responsibility, and collective action, educators and students can work together to achieve the goals of planetary education. Freire's vision of hope as a catalyst for empowerment and positive change reminds us of the potential of education to create a more just, equal, and sustainable future for all.

Seeds of Hope for the Pedagogy for Planetary *Convivência*

It is often believed that a giant hope is necessary to tackle society's immense problems. However, seeking and nurturing hope through small gestures and small acts of resistance can become a fundamental step to nurture hope in our lives. Cultivating small hopes through acts of love and kindness can

---

30. Conscientization, in Portuguese *conscientização*, is a structuring term in Freire's pedagogy. In *Pedagogy of the Oppressed*, he defines conscientization as the process of becoming aware of social, political, and economic contradictions in one's surroundings. This is not simply acknowledging unjust conditions while remaining passive, but rather, conscientization is an active effort to recognize these contradictions, reject them, and take action to overcome them. It involves both awareness of reality and engagement in the struggle to transform it.

be a consistent way to cope with feelings of hopelessness. These small pockets of resistance can also be delicate seeds that challenge a world full of grandiose projects and ideas. Today's society is confronted with numerous tragedies that can leave even the bravest of us feeling disenchanted with life and disillusioned with civic institutions. The abundant problems may lead some to feel indifferent and complacent. However, during times marked by discontent and unpredictability, it is more important than ever to view our circumstances through the lens of hope. This hope should be seen as a form of resistance that is not escapist or illusory. This hope should be a driving force inspiring us to strive for harmonious *convivência*.

Freire's emphasis on hope has motivated and inspired the making of his legacy. His insightful use of hope as an action verb, *esperançar*, different from the verb *esperar* (to wait)—which in Portuguese has the same root—became a distinctive element in his praxis and writings. Freire distinguished between true hope, which involves taking action and striving for change, and false hope, which means merely waiting for something to happen. So, this is the meaning of hope necessary for coping with today's adversities. True hope means getting up, going after, building, and never giving up. To hope is to move forward. To hope is to join with others to do otherwise.

Amorosidade/Lovingness as a Pedagogical Foundation

At the heart of Freire's philosophy lies another significant concept, "lovingness," which conveys a profound belief in the power of compassionate dialogue and empathy within educational contexts. Freire's philosophy of education is deeply rooted in humanization, liberation, and the rejection of oppressive pedagogical methods. His concept of lovingness, often described as an act of love, empathy, and genuine care for the learners, transcends traditional notions of instruction. Freire's emphasis on lovingness, or love—as an essential component of his pedagogy—is a theme that is often overlooked by most of his scholars. One of the exceptions is Antonia Darder, a critical educator and activist who sheds light on the significance of love in Freire's work. In her book *Freire and Education*, Darder explains how love pervades Freire's ideas in his language and actions. She argues that grasping the political nature of love is crucial to comprehending Freire's groundbreaking theory of conscientization and transformation. She emphasizes this saying, "Directly and indirectly, Freire touched on the essence of love as inseparable from our work as educators and democratic citizens of the world."[31]

Freire's lovingness implies a profound respect for learners' unique experiences and perspectives. He argues that educators should not impose knowledge onto students but instead engage in a reciprocal dialogue that encourages critical thinking, problem-posing, and collaborative exploration. Freire's commitment to a pedagogy of liberation, where students become active participants through a process of conscientization and, by extension, agents of social change, is made possible through loving relationships. According to Freire, love translated into mutual respect and kindness must be present in the relationships between teachers and students. The teacher's knowledge should not allow them to belittle the student's knowledge. Instead, the teacher should unconditionally respect the student as a human being with inherent dignity and help them to expand their critical perception of their reality. Darder explains,

> For Freire, the enactment of radical love in the classroom, in contrast, seeks to build a democratic field of critical praxis, in which numbing experiences of alienation can be openly named, challenged, and dismantled, creating a place for teachers and students to contend more honestly and effectively with human differences that exist between us, as we discard reactionary differences.[32]

The dimension of Freire's concept of love implies recognizing the need for dialogic action as an ethical foundation in pedagogical interactions. Therefore, he perceived the need for openness to the other through attentive and helpful dialogue as fundamental to human emancipation.

The Idea of *Amorosidade* in Paulo Freire

Throughout his life, Freire always used neologisms or expressions not used frequently in the Portuguese language to express his ideas more effectively. When addressing the theme of love in his writings, he chooses the word *amorosidade*, which means lovingness. The term *amorosidade* better encompasses the depth of his concept. Lovingness is a characteristic of those who express love, a quality of those who show love, a habit of those who are capable of loving and demonstrating it. For him, *amorosidade* possesses a

---

31. Darder, *Freire and Education*, 51.
32. Darder, *Freire and Education*, 58.

nuanced meaning. It's a human capability that materializes in the commitment to the other and the world. It involves humility and respect for the other. It means embracing the other. *Amorosidade*, as he said, is an act of courage. It requires trust. It also includes ethics that are based on everyday struggles. Furthermore, it expands beyond humans to include more-than-humans as he explains, "I don't believe in love between women and men, between human beings, if we don't become capable of loving the world. Ecology gains fundamental importance at the end of this century. It has to be present in any educational practice of a radical, critical and liberating nature."[33]

Amorosidade is more than acting cordially with someone; it also implies fully caring for others, abandoning oppressive attitudes, assuming a commitment to justice, and promoting the freedom that sustains the pact for life. Such loving-kindness extends to all created things. It constitutes the physical manifestation of a deep affection for people and the world that keeps people alive and engaged. The loving-kindness that materializes, engages, and problematizes reality through denunciation and announcement must be one of the guiding principles of emancipatory pedagogies. Freire says this world is not limited to the physical realm but includes our intentions and consciousness. It is a world of human connections built on historical and cultural influences, a world of love and affection. According to Freire, loving the world has a double meaning. It refers to the essential connection between the natural and sociocultural realms. Therefore, to love the world is to love every expression of life. This ethical dimension resonates profoundly with the goals of the pedagogy for planetary *convivência*, which seeks to instill values of justice, equity, and compassion in learners as they navigate an interconnected and diverse world.

The Ethics of *Amorosidade*

Amorosidade, in Freire's sense of the word, refers to the commitment we assume with the transformation of society through our pedagogical interventions, taking the cause of the oppressed in the boundaries of education. Thus, lovingness is necessary for educational relationships because sticking solely to technical-scientific competence and rigor denies the understanding of education as gnoseological. Therefore, lovingness encourages the

---

33. Freire, *Pedagogy of Indignation*, 47.

fundamental prerequisite for human coexistence and social conviviality. Freire asserts,

> What is important in teaching is not the mechanical repetition of this or that gesture but a comprehension of the value of sentiments, emotions, and desires . . . There is no true teaching preparation possible separated from a critical attitude that spurs ingenious curiosity to become epistemological curiosity, together with a recognition of the value of emotions, sensibility, affectivity, and intuition.[34]

Freire believes that it is unacceptable for teachers to lack love, care, and concern for their students. He argues that educators should demonstrate these qualities to their students and not fear being misunderstood. Technical-scientific competence and rigor are not incompatible with showing love and care during pedagogical interactions. Furthermore, for Freire, lovingness is just one of the indispensable virtues that critical educators must cultivate. Freire declares, "We need to know that, without certain qualities or virtues such as loving kindness, respect for others, tolerance, humility, taste for joy, taste for life, openness to the new, availability for change, persistence in the fight, rejection of fatalisms, identification with hope, openness to justice, the pedagogical-progressive practice is not possible, which is not done only with science and technique."[35] By aligning our minds and hearts, we can experience the true meaning of lovingness. Sensitive and emotional mobilization toward others and their historical condition is necessary for critical and ethical thinking. This integration of diverse knowledge paves the way for a more compassionate world. Moreover, when Freire talks about lovingness, he also wants to get us to think about how effectively our planet is loved, with its intricate biodiversity and unique position in the cosmos. So, such lovingness must also include our love for the world we inhabit and must be part of our efforts to increase our ecological awareness as part of a radical, critical, and liberating educational practice in favor of the Earth.

Amorosidade as a Praxis of Humanization

For Freire, *amorosidade* is linked to the praxis of humanization. This praxis is established in the dialogic relationships of the encounter between subjects

---

34. Freire, *Pedagogy of Freedom*, 48.

35. Freire, *Pedagogy of Freedom*, 108. The word *amorosidade* was translated as loving kindness from its original in Portuguese.

A Pedagogy for Planetary *Convivência*

and in the subject-world relationship. Authentic Freirean dialogue is governed by love, respect for what is different, and a belief in the horizontality of relationships between people for the construction of a fully democratic world. According to Freire, the vocation for humanization is a mark of human nature that is expressed in the quest to be more.

> Utopia, however, would not be possible if it lacked the taste for freedom that permeates the vocation for humanization. Or if it lacked hope, without which we do not struggle. The dream of humanization, whose concretization is always a process, and always a becoming, passes by way of breach with the real, concrete, economic, political, social, ideological, and so on, order, moorings that are condemning us to dehumanization. Thus the *dream* is a demand or condition that becomes ongoing in the history we make and that makes and remakes us.[36]

Lovingness is focused on the commitment to the other, respecting them in their differences and diversities. That's why, when oppressors dehumanize the oppressed, they also dehumanize themselves. As educators, we must deeply love the students and the educational process we are a part of. Without this love, we cannot truly fulfill our role as an educator.

Lovingness Within *Convivência* Pedagogy

Freire's concept of lovingness is particularly pertinent because an education promoting empathy, compassion, and a sense of responsibility toward the planet is urgently needed in a world dealing with social injustices, cultural divides, and ecological catastrophes. In its framework, lovingness enables students to comprehensively understand cultural diversity, ecological interdependence, and the inherent worth of all life forms. Freire's dialogical approach creates a space for learners to engage with different worldviews, perspectives, and experiences, cultivating a broader understanding of the complex web of relationships that shape and connect us to the planet. By fostering empathy and a deep sense of interconnectedness, lovingness contributes to forming environmentally conscious global citizens motivated to take collective action for the planet's well-being.

The pedagogy of planetary *convivência* encourages students to embrace active engagement with the problems facing the planet rather than merely acquiring an unresponsive understanding. Freire's dialogical

---

36. Freire, *Pedagogy of Hope*, 84.

approach, centered on lovingness, prepares learners to critically analyze complex global issues, such as climate change, resource depletion, and cultural conflicts, and obtain a sense of agency and responsibility to contribute to sustainable solutions and advocate for positive change on both local and planetary levels. As we grapple with pressing global challenges and seek to cultivate a sense of interconnectedness, empathy, and ethical responsibility, Freire's pedagogy of lovingness offers a transformative approach to education. By nurturing compassionate dialogue, critical consciousness, and a commitment to social justice, lovingness becomes a cornerstone for developing environmentally conscious global citizens. Therefore, in embracing Freire's vision of education as a force for liberation, empowerment, and social transformation, educators and learners can work together to create a more just, equitable, and sustainable world.

Ultimately, understanding the possible meaning of lovingness is more than trying to define it. It involves recognizing it as a historical need of humanity rooted in the world. This lovingness is not understood or assimilated as a banal feeling but rather an essential aspect of our duty to promote human expansiveness and advancement toward a more ethical society. We must strive to liberate ourselves from constrained notions of humanity and focus on building a society grounded in ethical principles. An education that distills and recovers the wisdom of spiritual and religious traditions can fill the void and help to form people who show respect to themselves, to others, and to the motherland. They become beings of compassion, love, and humility who work on behalf of humanity rather than for self-benefit or self-improvement. In a consumerist society, we have been convinced to have, or at least appear to have, the means to be considered a person. However, thinking without acknowledging others, the earth, and the Creator will not grant us the ability to be connected, belong, and live fully.

Dialogical Pedagogy: The Power of Dialogue

Freire's liberating education proposal has, in dialogue, one of the central characteristics of a critical and hopeful pedagogical project. Although this theme permeates all his writings, it is carefully analyzed in the *Pedagogy of the Oppressed*. In this book, Freire explores the concept of dialogue as a dialectic-problematizing process. According to Freire, the development of human subjectivity should be guided by ongoing dialogue with others and the ever-evolving reality that surrounds individuals. According to Freire, the dialogue goes beyond casual conversation and involves a respectful and collaborative exchange of ideas. Contrary to the traditional banking model of education, Freire's dialogical approach advocates for a problem-posing practice that values all voices and challenges the oppressive power dynamics within traditional education. Thus, dialogue is the means through which this transformation occurs. In the dialogical approach, teachers and students investigate the world together, and authentic dialogue occurs when everyone speaks and contributes to naming the world. Freire writes, "Dialogue is the encounter between men [and women], mediated by the world, in order to name the world. Hence, dialogue cannot occur between those who want to name the world and those who do not wish this naming—between those who deny others the right to speak their word and those whose right to speak has been denied them."[37]

Freire's educational philosophy maintains that education is an interactive process that encourages learners to think critically, to question, and to shape their realities. He expands on his dialogical framework by asserting that dialogue is essential for personal liberation and the transformation of society. He argues that dialogue is not just about one person sharing their ideas with another, nor is it simply about exchanging ideas. Instead, it is an existential necessity that goes beyond the individual. He states,

> Dialogue cannot be reduced to the act of one person's "depositing" ideas in another, nor can it become a simple exchange of ideas to be "consumed" by the discussants . . . Because dialogue is an encounter among women and men who name the world, it must not be a situation where some name on behalf of others. It is an act of creation; it must not serve as a crafty instrument for the domination of one person by another.[38]

In Freire's dialogical approach, certain conditions must be fulfilled to enable genuine dialogue to emerge. He believes that dialogue cannot exist without a profound love for the world and its inhabitants, humility, faith in humanity, hope, and solidarity. These factors work together to nurture a relationship built on trust and equality. He asserts, "Founding itself upon love, humility, and faith, dialogue becomes a horizontal relationship of which mutual trust between the dialoguers is the logical consequence. It would be a contradiction in terms if dialogue—loving, humble, and full of faith—did not produce this climate of mutual trust, which leads the

---

37. Freire, *Pedagogy of the Oppressed*, 69.
38. Freire, *Pedagogy of the Oppressed*, 70.

dialoguers into ever closer partnership in the naming of the world."[39] In the sequence, he emphasizes that having faith in humanity is a fundamental necessity for engaging in dialogue. However, trust is built through actively participating in discussions and connecting with others.[40]

Transformative Praxis: From Dialogue to Action

As espoused by Freire's dialogical pedagogy, the concept of transformative praxis places great emphasis on integrating theory and practice. Freire believes that dialogue is not an end goal but a means to encourage critical reflection and inspire concrete action. Dialogical action should prioritize the well-being and growth of individuals along the lines of *buen vivir* as discussed earlier, rather than merely conforming them to pre-established norms. This approach allows learners to become agents of change in their communities and beyond, bridging the gap between knowledge and action. The emphasis on praxis—the integration of theory and practice—in Freire's dialogical pedagogy is one of its distinguishing characteristics. In Freire's view, dialogue is not an end in itself but a means to provoke critical reflection and inspire concrete action. He declares, "Dialogue cannot exist, however, in the absence of a profound love for the world and for people. The naming of the world, which is an act of creation and re-creation, is not possible if it is not infused with love. Love is at the same time the foundation of dialogue and dialogue itself . . . If I do not love the world—if I do not love life—if I do not love people—I cannot enter into dialogue."[41] Freire's dialogical approach to education provides a compelling framework as we confront the urgent need for an education beyond borders, fostering empathy and inspiring learners to tackle pressing global issues.

Relevance of Dialogue to Pedagogy for Planetary *Convivência*

Freire's dialogical approach aligns with the principles of the pedagogy of planetary *convivência*, as it emphasizes problem-posing and critical thinking. Fostering collaboration and informed decision-making prepare individuals with the necessary skills to address complex global issues like

---

39. Freire, *Pedagogy of the Oppressed*, 72.
40. Freire, *Pedagogy of the Oppressed*, 72–73.
41. Freire, *Pedagogy of the Oppressed*, 70–71.

climate change and social inequality. By engaging in open and respectful dialogue with diverse individuals and communities, individuals can gain insights into different perspectives and challenge their assumptions and prejudices. Through open dialogue around pressing environmental issues, learners can develop a stronger connection to the natural world and better understand their role in preserving it. Striving to create a more equitable, sustainable, and interconnected world, educators and learners engage in dialogue, critical thinking, and transformative praxis work collaboratively for the betterment of humanity and the planet. However, these transformations should not occur within the school walls only. Since most schools are created within the capitalist structures within which they exist, we must seek to connect educational transformation with other social transformation that must concurrently take place at the workplace, through multiple social movements, communities of faith, and among other social constituencies.

Conscious citizens who recognize the planet as a shared home that requires careful stewardship can transcend individualism and nurture a sense of collective responsibility that acknowledges the interdependence of all life forms and ecosystems, thereby acquiring true planetary consciousness. By placing dialogue at the center of education, we are invited to reimagine it as a means of transformation, not just for individual liberation but also for nurturing a sense of responsibility and planetary awareness.

Solidarity as a Framework for Transformation

Another vital concept present in Freire's educational philosophy is solidarity. Solidarity, as defined by Freire, involves individuals coming together in unity, recognizing their shared humanity, and working collaboratively to address social injustices. Freire stresses respect for others, for those who are different, and solidarity actions as fundamental elements to form a critical consciousness of reality. According to him, individualism is the antithesis of solidarity because, from an individualistic perspective, each person thinks mainly about personal interests and tends to close in on oneself. Human existence is a political experience, declares Freire, and solidarity is a political and methodological issue that has to do with preparing ourselves to realize the dream of a transformed world. Thus, when we assume solidarity with people who are "disposable" in our societies, we carry out a political act.

Principles to *Sulear* Our Pedagogies

In the same way that when I am in solidarity with our planet, the land that welcomes us, the rivers that quench our thirst, and our ecosystem, I also exercise a political act. Sharing the fight to preserve the planet, human dignity, and fair relations between people is an act of solidarity. That is why solidarity is more than charity; it is an action that affects social structures. It is action; it is strength; it is that attitude of acceptance, of resistance capable of re-signifying our existence.

According to Freire, the necessary solidarity needs to be embraced by those who have similar dreams and not about a "society of angels" because angels do not make politics. Human beings do, and when they can come together in solidarity—to dream together and to struggle together for what they hope for—they can make changes.[42] Moreover, without solidarity and hope, it is impossible to struggle. Solidarity, then, occurs in the encounter between mind and hands, when the human body becomes a conscious body, and thus what to do in solidarity translates into being with the world and with others in this world.[43] Thus, solidarity is not a matter of sentiment but of action, of doing something for others to help them in their endeavors, and should inspire positive change. In the book *Pedagogy of Commitment*, Freire emphasizes that the critical educator's practice should be based on solidarity. He states, "As a function of and in response to our human condition, as conscious, curious, and critical beings, the educator's practice consists of fighting for a critical pedagogy that can give us tools to assert ourselves as the subjects of history. Such a practice must be based on solidarity."[44] Freire's pedagogy of solidarity challenges the banking model of education that stifles creativity and independent thought. Instead, he encourages educators and students to collaborate and exchange ideas and experiences. This type of education promotes solidarity and emphasizes the importance of having a positive impact on the world. Working collaboratively to construct knowledge and analyze social issues empowers individuals to effect change in their communities and society. This approach to education is transformative and emphasizes solidarity's active, transformative nature.

According to Freire, the only way to change the world is to perceive it from a perspective of solidarity. Freire says this is accomplished when there

---

42. Freire, *Pedagogy of Solidarity*, 62.
43. Freire, *Pedagogy of the Heart*, 33.
44. Freire, *Pedagogy of Commitment*, 14.

is harmony between what the mind thinks and what the hands do.[45] Therefore, being in the world implies being with the world and others. However, this is not a passive process. It requires actively combating oppression and striving for a better world for all.

Solidarity as an Ethical Commitment

Freire's concept of pedagogy of solidarity is rooted in a strong sense of ethics that goes beyond the classroom and extends to society. Freire emphasizes that solidarity requires a conscious and continuous effort to eliminate the barriers preventing individuals from being truly free. This statement highlights the inseparable connection between solidarity and the pursuit of justice, equality, and human rights. Educators who embrace the principle of solidarity are committed to facilitating learning, promoting social change, and addressing systemic inequalities. In the context of critical education, solidarity is not about charity. It is a journey of resistance and achievement, aiming to build a society founded on social responsibility, mutual support, and democratic connections. According to Freire, the ethics of solidarity among humans is the impetus that propels the struggle and generates innovative ideas to shape a more compassionate world. He argues,

> The historical, political, social, and cultural experience of men and women can never be acquired outside of the conflict between those forces that are dedicated to the prevention of self-assumption on the part of individuals and groups and those forces that work in favor of such an assumption . . . The socio-political solidarity that we need today to build a less ugly and less intolerant human community where we can be really what we are cannot neglect the importance of democratic practice.[46]

Solidarity is intrinsically linked to hope, *amorosidade*, and dialogue. Human solidarity is the driving force that feeds the resistance and creatively inspires the creation of a more humane world. The ethical aspect of this expansive notion of solidarity in Freire's teachings is in tune with the objectives of the pedagogy for planetary *convivência*. His focus on identifying the underlying causes of societal issues aligns with the goal of planetary

---

45. Freire, *Pedagogy of the Heart*, 33.
46. Freire, *Pedagogy of Freedom*, 46.

education aiming to confront the ecological and social challenges that endanger the well-being of present and future generations.

Solidarity within Planetary Pedagogy

Freire's concept of solidarity assumes particular relevance in the context of the pedagogy for planetary *convivência*, which seeks to cultivate a sense of interconnectedness, environmental concerns, and intercultural understanding. Considering the current global challenges we face, such as climate change, resource depletion, terrorism, the migration crisis, diseases, debt, and economic insecurity, among many others, it is crucial to adopt a pedagogical approach that transcends borders and nurtures a sense of collective responsibility. Freire's conception of solidarity is appropriate to these goals, providing a framework for cultivating environmental and planetary consciousness. Freire stresses the importance of solidarity in bringing about social change. He argues that to be in solidarity with others, one must fully immerse themselves in their situation, which requires a radical mindset. This involves showing empathy, being actively involved, and having courage to challenge unjust systems. Solidarity, more than just a theoretical concept, is a powerful force that can drive real action and bring about positive change. It's not just an act of generosity but a matter of justice.

In the framework of the Pedagogy for Planetary *Convivência* context, solidarity is crucial in encouraging learners to appreciate diverse cultural perspectives, recognize the interdependence of ecosystems, and take action on environmental and social justice issues. Solidarity, as emphasized by Freire, plays a crucial role in planetary education. By engaging in dialogue and cooperation, students can acquire a more profound comprehension of intricate global problems and foster the ability to analyze and tackle these issues. This critical consciousness enables students to challenge dominant perspectives and unsustainable practices and contemplate alternative routes toward a more just and sustainable world.

The Pedagogy of Planetary *Convivência* can use the power of solidarity to motivate learners to take action in an informed and meaningful way. Through working together on projects, promoting policy changes, and joining global initiatives, learners demonstrate the values of solidarity as they tackle essential environmental and social issues. This approach to education corroborates with the vision of education as a tool for empowerment and liberation, enabling learners to actively contribute to creating a more viable and fairer world. Hence, solidarity is a powerful tool for promoting global citizenship and recognizing the interdependence that must exist to guarantee a habitable planet and its inhabitants. With the complex challenges we face today, solidarity can be a guiding principle toward collective solutions. By engaging in empathetic conversations, developing critical awareness, and taking ethical action, students can become agents of positive change in their communities and beyond. By embracing solidarity, both educators and students can play a role in building a just, viable, and compassionate world. I believe that our task as critical educators—involved in the construction of another possible world—cannot be carried out in isolation but needs to be part of a solidary effort in the fight for autonomy, justice and democracy.

In conclusion, in this process of *sulear* our pedagogies, we will need to adopt pedagogical styles that horizontalize our interactions. However, horizontalization will not occur outside the social, political, and economic institutions where we participate and exercise our pedagogical praxis. We cannot imagine that our job as critical educators will be to love everyone, and that, magically, democracy and justice will emerge. We need committed and courageous actions to combat the educational process that perpetuates a rationality that excludes everything that is not logical and measurable and in accordance with Western standards with their self-validating and self-referential languages that present themselves as unquestionable. We certainly need logical skills, but we also need emotional ones. As the latter is out of step with the dominant school model, we must develop, nurture, and strengthen these capabilities to thrive and achieve positive changes. All humans possess the ability to love, care, and to demonstrate solidarity and compassion. However, these abilities may not continuously be fully developed and, thus, require education and nurturing to thrive and make positive changes. Planetary *convivência* is a laborious construction that involves a relationship with all humans and more-than-humans. While we can never fully achieve this goal due to the inherent limitations of our existence, we must seek a better way to live with one another. We can create a more supportive community by cultivating empathy and expressing kindness and compassion.

6

A Pedagogy Otherwise
Cartography of Affections

> Caminante, no hay camino, se hace camino al andar.
> Al andar se hace el camino, y al volver la vista atrás
> se ve la senda que nunca se ha de volver a pisar.
> Caminante, no hay camino sino estelas en la mar.
>
> —Antonio Machado[1]

Mapping Our Inner Landscape

EVERYTHING AND EVERYONE ARE an indispensable part of the cosmos. The path we take on our planetary journey is the one we make as we walk, as Antonio Machado poetically expressed it. However, we don't walk alone; "We walk in constellations," says Ailton Krenak.[2] In this journey, our task is to prevent our constellations from becoming impenetrable. By refusing interactions with other constellations, we will lose the opportunity to be mutually enriched and expanded.

---

1. Antonio Machado Ruiz, born in Seville, is considered one of the 20th-century's most outstanding poets. Free translation. Traveler, there is no road; you make your path as you walk. As you walk, you make your own road, and when you look back, you see the path you will never travel again. Traveler, there is no road; only a ship's wake on the sea.

2. Krenak. *A Vida Não é Útil* (Life Is not Useful), 39.

A Pedagogy for Planetary *Convivência*

On this journey that is our life, we walk with fellow travelers, those we know, and with others who are strangers to us. We also walk with those who came before us, whom we carry in our DNA, in our cherished memories, and through their legacies that we seek to preserve within us. This has to do with our biological and social structure as human beings. When life's journey becomes chaotic, instead of giving up, we should continue our journey by learning to work on how *to suspend the sky*.[3] In other words, when we are aware that a colonial project is still ongoing, and has been intentionally designed to bury plural cosmologies, we need to rescue rituals to inspire our creativity and boost our ability to *dis-orient* such systems, thus helping us to *sulear* our lives by using different sources of wisdom.

For instance, Aitlon Krenak describes how dreams allow the Krenak people to connect cosmic reality and everyday life by guiding the lives of hunters and farmers in a harmonious relationship with nature. They observe the sky's motion and how it interacts with the earth. They can recognize, then, when they have disconnected themselves from other living beings. So, when they feel that the pressure of the heaven is exceptionally close to the earth, they believe that it is time to perform the ritual of singing and dancing, with the intention of suspending the sky. This ceremony is carried out at the start of spring. He says, "So, it is necessary to dance and sing to suspend it [the sky], so that the changes related to the health of the Earth and of all beings happen in this passageway. When we do the *taru andé*, this ritual, it means communion with the web of life that gives us power."[4]

Suspending the sky means expanding horizons, dreaming other dreams, and creating other bonds of affection so that we can embrace the world otherwise. The emphasis placed by Eurocentric epistemologies on mental processes ignores the importance of emotions, feelings, and subjectivity, which are integral to our existence as beings of connection. For this reason, we often construct knowledge while being disconnected from our bodies and other ways of understanding and experiencing reality. Indigenous cultures teach us to *see with our hearts* and to *think with our feet*. Such an approach of seeing the world and learning about our existence through all the senses has the potential to return us to our fundamental nature as beings of relationships and affections.

While most academics agree that learning requires collaboration, this process often doesn't happen cooperatively—in the company of others.

---

3. Krenak. *A Vida Não é Útil*, 45.
4. Krenak. *A Vida Não é Útil*, 46.

A Pedagogy Otherwise

Most of the time, we continue to learn on our own, not *with* others. Such an individualistic attitude is intentionally designed by an educational system that continues to colonize our minds, bodies, and emotions. Sometimes, we recognize the importance of the time-space and the contexts where knowledge is constructed, but we pay less attention to emotional reactions that aid or hinder learning as if it were possible to experience life "wearing gloves and masks," as Donaldo Macedo reminds us.[5] When real emotions touch our lives, we try to sublimate them by sanitizing the learning process to avoid contamination by other ways of knowing. By choosing to wear gloves and masks, we try to cover up the human attempt to avoid contradictory feelings, which reveals the struggle between *symbállein* and *diaballein* in our interpersonal interactions.[6] We prefer to remain sheltered behind cognitive shields rather than adventure ourselves through uncharted territories. We try to get involved in the learning process as if it were possible to do it without co-inspiring, without feeling each other's heartbeat, and without savoring the magnificence of life that unfolds before our eyes as we contemplate the beauty of the sunset, the vivid colors of the flowers, the symphony of the birds, the splendor of the rivers, the expanse of the blue ocean, the cozy shadows of the trees, and the mysteries of the forests.

In *Pedagogy of Hope*, Freire recounts a time when he was experiencing overwhelming feelings of sadness. At that period in his life, he longed for the familiar scents of wet earth, the sun's warmth, the lush tropical foliage, and cherished memories of his childhood. Being separated from his loved ones for so long during his exile had taken its toll on him. In doing this exercise of remembering, Freire saw the importance of it. He says, "That rainy afternoon, with the sky dark as lead over the bright green land, the ground soaked, I discovered the fabric of my depression. I became conscious of various relationships between the signs and the central core, the deeper core, hidden within me. I unveiled the problem by clearly and lucidly grasping its 'why.' I dug up the archaeology of my pain."[7] As Nita Freire explains,[8] he used the term figuratively to refer to the "archaeology" he did on his past feelings while conducting an in-depth analysis, a genuine excavation of the emotions that led to his suffering and depression. Freire's motivation to do an archeology of his pain helped him to better understand the feelings

---

5. Freire, *Pedagogy of Freedom*, xii.
6. See chapter *Buen Vivir,* 38.
7. Freire, *Pedagogy of Hope*, 22.
8. Freire, *Pedagogy of Hope*, 197.

that made him hostage and immobilized by laying bare the web in which the facts occurred and, thus, discovering their reason for being. By doing this process of inner journey, he could break limit-situations, overcoming barriers that limit him from *being more.*

As human beings, we often avoid this challenging archaeological exercise because we may not see its value or necessity. While we've made significant strides in science, technology, robotics, and information technology, we still don't know how to access these painful and stressful places within ourselves. The truth is, we prefer to avoid facing our deepest wounds. The unbridled search for survival in the face of an individualizing and competitive ethic has often led us to shy away from looking within ourselves with the illusion that if material needs are met, other needs will be satisfied. However, human beings are not just biological structures. We are emotional beings capable of feeling, desiring, and establishing relationships with each other for our survival. Yet, sometimes, we use reason to justify or hide our emotions. Of course, we cannot and should not discard our reason, but we must understand it based on the intertwining relationship between our reason and feelings. We are beings of connections, and through the mental habits we preserve, the relationships we establish, and the spirituality we cultivate, we give meaning to our existence. That's why archeologizing our emotions can help us understand our feelings more clearly and without subterfuge.

Archaeologizing our Emotions

Archaeology generally involves investigating the history, past and present, of humanity through physical evidence. However, archaeology is much more than just exploring ancient artifacts. It involves diving deep into human history to gain insight into our ancestors' lives, beliefs, practices, and innovations. Through the meticulous study of artifacts, structures, and landscapes, archaeology helps unravel the mysteries of past civilizations and fosters a thorough understanding of human evolution. Contemporary societies can learn valuable lessons about sustainable practices by studying how ancient civilizations adapted to changing climates and landscapes. Archaeologists utilize ancient materials to inform the conservation and restoration of historic sites, ensuring that future generations connect with their cultural heritage.

Freire's suggested use of archaeology as a metaphor offers insights into the human condition and our connection to time and emotions.

Archaeological work involves unearthing and analyzing layers of accumulated residues, offering a glimpse into how the events and memories that shape our identity accumulate over time. These layers serve as a record of our past, revealing the stories of our ancestors and the civilizations that came before us. In this sense, archaeology serves as a metaphor for the process of self-discovery and understanding to unravel the essence of our shared humanity.

As we excavate the layers of our experiences, we unveil past events and gain a deeper understanding of our place in the intricate web of life. We realize that we are "caught in an inescapable web of mutuality," as Martin Luther King Jr. put it. With this understanding, we can expand our perspective to unearth the stories of those who came before us, reminding us that our current struggles and triumphs are part of an ongoing narrative that extends far beyond our lives. Examining our emotions through the metaphor of archaeology in the context of education involves recognizing what feelings we hide or suppress during educational exchanges, especially when we are subject to a model of education that stifles, compartmentalizes, and despises our emotions. This open reflection can lead us not only to map our emotions, but also to embrace a necessary cartography of affections.

Cartography of Affections

In his book *Futuro Ancestral* (Ancestral Future), Ailton Krenak proposes the concept of a "cartography of affections," which complements Freire's idea of exploring our emotions and pain through archaeological assessment. Krenak encourages us to imagine a world of "cartography, layers of worlds, in which the narratives are so plural that we don't need to come into conflict when evoking different foundation stories."[9] He believes these stories are significant to individual experiences in various life contexts. The author suggests we consider the "worlds of affective cartography,"[10] which for him encompass humanity and the biodiversity of the Earth, including rivers, vegetation, and animals. I find his idea about the "cartography of affections" inspiring and in line with the principles for pedagogy that I propose, which emphasizes empathy and interconnection to promote *planetary convivência*.

---

9. Krenak, *Futuro Ancestral*, 32.
10. Krenak, *Futuro Ancestral*, 42.

Although cartography has been subject to controversy due to its history of being used as a tool for colonization, causing harm to indigenous communities, even in modern times, a chance exists for understanding it in a decolonial framework. By showcasing or reviving worlds beyond the colonial mindset, it is possible to use it to combat neocolonial cartographies, as highlighted by the authors of the special edition of the International Journal "Cartographica." Through the insightful articles, the authors provide an overview of the theory and praxis of decolonial mapping, and in the summary of the edition: "For over five centuries, cartographic map-making has played a pivotal role as a political technology of empire-building, settler colonialism, and the dispossession of Indigenous lands. Yet Indigenous peoples themselves have long engaged in their own mapping practices to share ancestral knowledge, challenge colonial rule, and reclaim Indigenous 'place-worlds.'"[11] As the authors indicate, cartographies go beyond just physical spaces on maps. Seen from an expansive perspective, they include historical, social, and cultural aspects that reflect different epistemologies and incorporate all dimensions of life that can reveal people's ways of being and engaging with the world. Mapmaking from a decolonial perspective is a powerful reminder that the true essence of a place cannot be fully encapsulated within the confines of paper and ink, instead it can be described as a delicate dance between representation and distortion. As wondrous as their depictions may be, they are but crafted tales, imperfect echoes of the vast and intricate reality they seek to portray.

Following Krenak's proposal to create cartographies of affection, I argue for the need to map the emotional landscape in educational environments. By embracing this idea, we can facilitate the development of affective connections that positively impact pedagogical interactions, educating individuals to be more empathetic and involved with their communities. A cartography of affections can venture us into the intricate territories of human emotions and attachments in a data-driven world. Thus, in the same way that a map illustrates the physical terrain, the cartography of affections delves into the complex realm of feelings, thoughts, and relationships. It sheds light on the complexities of our inner landscape and has profound implications for a pedagogy for *convivência*—a pedagogy aimed at nurturing holistic growth and critical consciousness.

---

11. Rose-Redwood et al., "Decolonizing the Map: Recentering Indigenous Mappings," 151.

A Pedagogy Otherwise

The mapping of emotions is closely tied to Freire's educational approach and the epistemologies of the Global South. I concur with Antonia Darder that Freire can be seen as an early epistemologist from the South,[12] as his epistemological sensibilities challenge the oppressive structures of power. In addressing the issues of his time, Freire urges his readers to resist the pressures of Western academicism, which he refers to as a banking model education, proposing a liberation education aiming to close the abyssal divide characteristic of Western epistemologies. According to Boaventura de Sousa Santos, the abyssal line refers to the boundary separating social reality into two distinct parts. Anything that falls on one side of this line is visible and considered relevant. In contrast, anything that falls on the other side of this line is either invisible or considered irrelevant. Much in line with Freire's positions, Santos argues that the epistemologies of the South focus on validating knowledge based on the experiences of marginalized groups who have suffered from injustices, oppression, and destruction due to capitalism, colonialism, and patriarchy.[13] For Freire, liberation education connects emotions, body, knowledge, and the struggle to overcome oppression. He says that it is the body that writes, speaks, fights, loves, and hates. It is the body that suffers and dies, and it is the body that lives.[14]

The body, a territory of knowledge, memories, and experience, is also a political territory from which emancipation and freedom can emerge. In another passage, Freire states: "I know with my whole body, with feelings, with passion and also with reason."[15] For him, such emotions are not the result of sentimentality, but of a consistent commitment to the liberation of oppressed bodies, because it is through the body that one names the world and pronounces her word. That is why banking education systematically silences voices and makes them malleable bodies. In a liberating perspective of education, bodies are seen as places of resistance against a pedagogy of rigidity and denial of affection. Reframing the body as a pedagogical territory expands the possibilities for articulating collective knowledge and memories, including ancestral wisdom and recognizing the construction of knowledge based on coexistence with other bodies.

As Eduardo Galeano says, "education chops us into pieces: it teaches us to divorce soul from body and mind from heart." In opposition to such

---

12. Darder, *The Student Guide to Freire's Pedagogy of the Oppressed*, ix.
13. Sousa Santos, *The End of the Cognitive Empire*, 1–35.
14. Freire and Faundez, *Por uma pedagogia da pergunta*, 29.
15. Freire, *Pedagogy of the Heart*, 30.

attempt, he reminds that the Colombian fishermen are doctors of ethics and morality, for they personified the "marriage of heart and mind" and invented the term *sentipensante*—feeling-thinking—to define language that speaks the truth.[16]

Colombian sociologist Orlando Fals Borda also admires the ancient practice of "thinking with one's heart and feeling with one's head."[17] Borda is credited with coining the term *sentipensar*. Still, he recognizes on many occasions that he learned it from the culture of the Colombian Caribbean people and, more specifically, the riverside culture of the Rio Grande de La Magdalena. The riverside people taught him the concept of "Hicotea Man." When facing life's setbacks, the "Hicotea man" withdraws for a while, only to reappear with the same vigor afterward. The feeling-thinking man who combines reason and love, body and heart, to destroy all evil that shatters this harmony is the one who is capable of telling the truth.[18] The concept of *sentipensar*—which in Freire can be understood as the impossibility of the false dichotomy between thinking and feeling—makes it possible to overcome the binary separations between feeling and thought, body and mind. It outlines other ways of conceiving and being *in* and *with* the world. Therefore, acknowledging and appreciating people's emotions is essential to valuing and recognizing their unique and complex nature. Seeing the world and learning through all the senses returns us to our fundamental nature as relational beings.

I suggest that the cartography of affections serves as a bridge between the emotional and cognitive domains. By making emotions visible and tangible, learners can explore the emotional underpinnings of their experiences, fostering a deeper understanding of themselves and others. This approach fosters interpersonal skills, emotional intelligence, and empathy—all of which are necessary for both individual and community well-being. The liberating education expounded by Freire seeks to foster critical consciousness, which encompasses a deep understanding of the social, political, and cultural factors that impact our existence not only cognitively but emotionally. Embracing the cartography of affections in our educational task will add to Freire's vision, because by mapping our emotions we will

---

16. Galeano, *The Book of Embraces*, 121.

17. Borda is recognized as a trailblazer in participatory action research, where individuals or groups collaborate in generating knowledge. His *sentipensante* sociology is based on the expertise of marginalized communities in Colombia, who, like many others worldwide, are the primary targets of violence.

18. Borda, *Una sociología sentipensante*, 9–10.

be able to better understand how social, political, and cultural factors affect us in many ways. Awareness of one's emotions can help individuals authentically express themselves in learning environments and develop the ability to analyze societal norms, power structures, and systemic inequalities from their hearts and not only their minds. A pedagogy that promotes emotional self-expression has the potential to create a supportive community where people can connect on a deeper and more genuine level.

The cartography of affections can guide learners through the intricate labyrinth of emotions, illuminating the way to a more enlightened and empathetic existence. In a world where the cacophony of information often drowns out the heart's whispers, this approach invites us to embark on an inner journey, an expedition into feelings and emotions. However, embarking on an adventure of introspection requires courage to embrace vulnerability. As individuals traverse their emotional landscapes, both instructors and students will encounter emotions that may have been repressed, desires that have not been mapped and wounds that are still open. Mapping these emotions becomes an empowering process revealing that the emotions are real, legitimate, and meaningful.

Just as earthly cartography guides travelers through the physical world, the cartography of affection can guide us through the complexities of the heart, fostering a deeper understanding of ourselves and our purpose in the cosmos. Through the imaginative movements of emotional mapping, individuals gain insight into the nuances of their emotional landscape. They can recognize the peaks and valleys of their feelings, the hidden sources of joy, the turbulent rivers of anger, and the tranquil meadows of contentment. When heightened, this self-awareness can empower students to respond to their emotions more intentionally and constructively, moving them away from reactionary behavior and toward thoughtful and empathetic responses. However, we must remember that we have been educated to hide our emotions, so this path will not be easy, and it is not ready. It is a path that will be made by walking. Because it is a path still under construction, we will inevitably have to undo and abandon many of the old habits that have led us astray from our true selves.

By exploring our emotions, we embark on a shared journey of discovery, gaining a deeper understanding of what it means to be human in all its complexity. This journey should help us break down barriers between people and foster solidarity as we realize that our emotional experiences are universal and interconnected. When people understand and appreciate each other's emotional journeys, they are better equipped to engage in meaningful dialogue, resolve conflict, and co-create a more resilient community. Similar to physical landscapes that change and develop over time, emotional landscapes also evolve, and sometimes acknowledging them can be painful. Just as physical cartographers face uncharted territories and confusing terrain, emotional cartography can face obstacles, contradictions, and moments of uncertainty. However, as individuals continually update and refine their emotional maps, they engage in an ongoing process of self-discovery and personal growth. This transformative journey reminds us that the path to self-knowledge is never linear but rather circular. As a principle of the natural world, circularity is organic. It is always in motion, as seen in the changes of the seasons, the life-death-life cycle, and the waters that fall as rain, evaporate, and fall again. The terrains of emotions are not a uniform or clearly delineated space, but a dynamic, ever-changing, and beautifully imperfect mosaic. Ultimately, the cartography of affections can enable us to navigate the complex landscapes of the heart, fostering a deeper connection with ourselves, others, and the world, allowing a re-signification of our experiences and emotions.

Within the scope of pedagogy for planetary *convivência*, emotional mapping goes beyond the limits of the classroom and achieves social transformation, as empathetic connections have the power to heal our bodies and restore our souls. An emotionally intelligent society embraces diversity, honors individual narratives, and dismantles prejudices. A lack of empathy would be detrimental to *convivência* because it would prevent us from responding to the most resounding cries of our hearts. However, *convivência*, as expounded here, cannot be forced; it must be fostered. It must be developed and learned through actions. In fact, such an effort can be challenging because it requires humility, simplicity, complicity, commitment, mutual understanding, patience, solidarity, time and, above all, love and tenderness. Living together, whether in a family, neighborhood, or public space, means sharing dreams, hopes, joys, but also difficulties and disappointments. *Convivência* is a learning process that teaches us to understand one another, share spaces and responsibilities, pursue goals, nurture hopes, face limitations, and work through challenges collaboratively. It means commitment not only to human beings but also to the planet.

The perspective of the Pedagogy for Planetary *Convivência* described here is still imperfect, as are the maps. However, despite not being able to fully grasp the full breadth and depth of the pedagogical territories it portrays, it glimpses the essence of the cartography of affections in their contours, by encouraging empathy, emotional intelligence and interpersonal skills—essential for personal and social well-being. In addition, within the scope of the pedagogy of *convivência*, showing affection is a way of resisting the rigidity of relationships, the denial of feelings, and the standardization of behaviors. Such pedagogy embraces a decolonial view of the world because it takes a stand against the mechanisms that try to chain our bodies, muffle our mouths, and imprison our gestures.

Even though there is proof that our predecessors were aggressive, they were also kind and compassionate people. For Chilean philosopher and neurobiologist Humberto Maturana, life on the planet has been sustained not by the survival of the fittest, but by cooperation among living beings. He argues that competition is antisocial because it involves the denial of others. For him, discarding love as the biological basis of social life means going back in a history of living beings that is more than 3.5 million years old. He argues:

> Hence, the only possibility for coexistence is to opt for a broader perspective, a domain of existence in which both parties fit in the bringing forth of a common world . . . This act is called love, or, if we prefer a milder expression, the acceptance of the other person beside us in our daily living. This is the biological foundation of social phenomena: without love, without acceptance of others living beside us, there is no social process and, therefore, no humanness.[19]

According to Maturama, love is the only emotion that expands intelligence, and this is because intelligence is essentially accepting the legitimacy of the other and expanding the potential for consensuality that results from that acceptance. We only remain *homo sapiens amans* if love continues to be a central emotion in the systemic preservation of our unique human identity, for if we engage life through competition and aggressiveness, we will become *Homo sapiens aggressans*.[20] If we admit such a statement, what more revolutionary attitude could there be than love translated into words and attitudes of affection?

Love is a subversive force that impels us to meet others, and that is translated into gestures of affection and tenderness. In times of artificial intelligence, we need to be attentive and aware of what things can humanize

---

19. Maturama and Varela, *The Tree of Knowledge*, 246.
20. Maturama, *Transformación en la Convivencia*, 226–27.

or robotize us. Machines can't love or show affection; They do not weep in the face of the beautiful or the tragic. They may become more intelligent than humans, but they won't have a heart.

In life, we encounter a variety of situations and challenges that require us to be attentive and responsive. To navigate through life's ups and downs, it is crucial to cultivate sensitive reasoning. This means that we must be open to perceiving the signs and signals that come to us from different sources, whether they be from our intuition, other people, or external events. By developing our capacity for sensitive reasoning, we can better understand the world around us and make informed decisions that serve our well-being. We must rescue the sensibility in all its pulsating dimensions that generate life and a sense of belonging, for it is not machines, progress, or technology that will unite us. Our decision to come together, to meet the other and exchange ideas, to explore new paths and rehearse new harmonies, however dissonant they may be, is what will bring us together and enable us of cultivating a pedagogy for planetary *convivência*.

The Colombian psychiatrist and philosopher Luis Carlos Restrepo, in his book *El Derecho a la Ternura*, (*The Right to Tenderness*) reflects on the pedagogical and social demands of our brain: "Without a doubt, the brain needs hugs for its development, and the most important cognitive structures depend on this affective food to reach an adequate level of competence. We must not forget, as Leontiev demonstrated several years ago, that the brain is an authentic social organ in need of environmental stimuli for its development. Without an affective matrix, the brain cannot reach its highest heights in the adventure of knowledge."[21]

As Restrepo suggests, bringing tenderness into everyday life requires a sensory investment accessing, as in the rituals of meaningful initiation, a condition of modification of consciousness that forces us to go beyond the boundaries that have imprisoned our system of knowledge.[22] For him, demonstrations of affection can even influence our immune system because these, when lacking, put our existence at risk and deteriorate our health. Tenderness is the result of accepting ourselves as unfinished and fragmented beings, and this recognition allows the emergence of a logic of interdependence and sensitivity essential to entering a world without the desire for conquest. In another book, Restrepo affirms:

---

21. Restrepo, *El Derecho a la Ternura*, 50 (free translation).
22. Restrepo, *El Derecho a la Ternura*, 51.

A Pedagogy Otherwise

> We believe it is possible to overcome emotional illiteracy, so that the conflict between dependence and singularity does not become a source of unnecessary suffering. For this, it is a priority to learn to take care of our emotional niches from the pollution and contamination derived from the excess of functional dialogues and the presence of emotional intimidation in the interpersonal world. A path that we can travel by making pacts of tenderness understood as an ethical position that provides criteria to address the inevitable clash between dependence and singularity.[23]

For this pedagogy of *convivência* to flourish, it is necessary to develop a loving and planetary consciousness through in which new forms of educational relationships are collectively created. Thus, in the interweaving of ideas and feelings, we can imagine what is not yet visible, but is possible. Because we are contradictory beings—beings of love and care, but also violent, predatory, and perverse beings—any positive social change we aim to achieve requires an alignment between our decisions, attitudes, and desires aiming at a *buen vivir* for everyone.

The imperative to build a pedagogy for planetary *convivência* becomes increasingly urgent in the contemporary planetary landscape that is characterized by the brutal reality of the extermination of entire peoples and communities, a scenario that is undoubtedly bleak. Elaborating a pedagogy that defends *planetary convivência* may initially seem daunting, if not unattainable, task, especially when overshadowed by the skepticism and discouragement prevalent in social spheres. However, like river springs that join other waterways at successive confluences until they flow into the banks of the main river, there is a source of hope amid these challenges. In this source lies an inherent resilience that points us forward, toward the utopia in the Freirean sense. Freire believes in the transformation of reality through the fulfillment of conceivable dreams that are currently in progress.

The pedagogy that prioritizes planetary *convivência* is not a mere theoretical abstraction. It is a practical response to the pressing need for a change in consciousness and collective action to face humanity's profound challenges. Its need arises within the walls of pessimism, cynicism, and disillusionment generated by widespread fear and disrespect. However, precisely within these walls, we must deliberately look for the gaps and fissures in the impenetrable veneer of current reality, through which we can uncover possible paths to a more compassionate *convivência*.

---

23. Restrepo, *Ecologia Humana*, 5 (free translation).

A Pedagogy for Planetary *Convivência*

Finding and sharing inspiring accounts of resilience and hope that are sometimes overlooked in the shadow of widespread hopelessness is essential to navigating the landscape of *planetary convivência*. These narratives act as encouragements, shedding light on the potential for revolutionary change and igniting a new sense of direction. Teachers and activists are urged to become storytellers, not reproducers of a single story. Our textbooks, curricula, and pedagogies need to contain and tell stories other than that of the winners. It is impossible to continue to tell a "single story," as Chimamanda Ngozi Adichie[24] insightfully demonstrates. We cannot continue to accept and teach the narrative of the Discovery of the Americas without talking about the *encubrimiento de las Americas* (the concealment of the Americas) as Enrique Dussel[25] refers to it. For him, the other was not discovered as the Other but was covered up through a process of concealment of the non-European. Such a process triggers dehumanization because the other comes to be seen as the enemy, undesirable, and less than others, which reinforces xenophobic and racist perspectives.

The pedagogy for planetary *convivência* must tell stories from different places and peoples that inspire us to honor deeds of kindness, environmental care, and cultural preservation. By participating in collective resistance, we can actively work towards a more sustainable and interconnected future. By engaging in this process, we can envision the pedagogy for planetary *convivência* not as a conceptual framework, but as a lived experience. This will allow us to have a more constructive approach towards it. This will pave the way for a future in which recognizing the diversity and interconnectedness of all life and its interdependence can replace indifference and violence.

Based on the principles set out in the previous chapter, in order to cultivate such a pedagogy, we cannot outsource our emotions. We need to embrace hope to improve our *convivência*. We need love to fuel our creativity. We need dialogue to strengthen our ideas and amplify them. We need solidarity to manifest our gestures of tenderness. Expanding on these principles, it becomes evident that the foundation of pedagogy for *planetary convivência* and, indeed, our entire social fabric must rest on a fundamental acceptance of love, hope, dialogue, and solidarity.

Hope is the guiding force that propels us forward, instigating positive change and fostering an environment conducive to growth and learning.

---

24. Adichie, "The Danger of a Single Story."
25. Dussel, *1492 El Encubrimiento del Otro*.

A Pedagogy Otherwise

When we feel loved, appreciated, and valued, our minds tend to be more open, receptive, and imaginative. Dialogue plays a fundamental role in shaping the contours of our ideas, refining them and, when necessary, rectifying them and reaffirming what is valid. It serves as an incubator where many points of view intersect and germinate, creating a vibrant intellectual conversation that goes beyond the boundaries of individual understanding. Through meaningful dialogue, we not only strengthen our own convictions, but also cultivate a more robust and resilient collective intelligence. This collaborative process of refining ideas through dialogue ensures that our educational methodologies remain contextual, relevant, and responsive to the evolving needs of a diverse and dynamic society. Solidarity emerges as the axis that manifests our gestures of tenderness. In the educational context, solidarity means a shared commitment to the well-being and success of each participant in the learning journey. It involves extending support, understanding difficulties, and collectively celebrating achievements. Solidarity transforms pedagogy into a communal endeavor, where the successes of one become the triumphs of all, fostering a sense of unity and interconnectedness. Ultimately, weaving the threads of hope, love, dialogue, and solidarity into the fabric of our pedagogical approaches is essential to creating an educational environment that is not only intellectually stimulating but also emotionally nurturing. These principles are the cornerstone of our commitment to cultivating a society where learning is a transformative and compassionate journey in which individuals united generate growth, understanding, and mutual respect.

A colonial pedagogy is a pedagogy of imprisonment, oppression and violence against bodies and minds. It is a pedagogy of extermination. Its language is linear and seeks to inhibit and immobilize people. On the other hand, pedagogy for *convivência,* it is a pedagogy of dialogue, of open space for differences, for belonging and for solidarity. Its language is circular, it is engaging, it is of everyone and for everyone. It is anti-colonial and decolonial. It is biophilic and not catechetical; it is *sentir—pensar—agir* pedagogy (feeling-thinking-acting).

The pedagogy of and for planetary *convivência* is a place for the untested feasibility—what is not yet—to emerge in the affective encounter with others based on their ethical-aesthetic sense. It is a pedagogy that seeks to break with the framework of the colonial project and hopes to make each person, especially those from the peripheries of the world *to be more,* which in the Freirean sense means overcoming the limit situations that imprison people physically and mentally. Limit-situations become opportunities to adjust our focus, to expand our boundaries, to regain our strength for the struggles. Freire expressed his sentiment in constant defense of the conviction that, if it is possible to fight collectively, it is also possible to win collectively. Thus, his choice has an ideological nature, betting on the validity of the concept of the untested feasibility. Nita Freire says: "The 'untested feasibility' then, when all is said and done, is something the utopian dreamer knows exists, but know that it will be attained only through a practice of liberation—which can be implemented by way of Freire's theory of dialogical action, or, of course (since the practice of liberation does not necessarily make an explicit appeal to that theory), by way of some other theory bearing on the same ends."[26] She adds, the "untested feasibility" is in fact something that is not yet clearly known, but dreamed of by those who think utopically, and who know that it can become reality.

In the spirit of Paulo Freire's teachings, this term "untested feasibility" encapsulates the radical belief that what has not been tried or proven feasible within existing frameworks can in fact be accomplished through collective effort and determination. By asserting that there are unrealized opportunities and unrealized potentials within the reach of the achievable, it challenges the current status quo that denies freedom. By embracing untested feasibility, this pedagogy invites participants to envision and actively seek out alternatives that may have been discarded or neglected within conventional educational paradigms. It's not a method of transmitting knowledge; rather, it is a conscious choice to fight for justice, equality, and emancipation. The praxis of this pedagogy reveals a firm commitment to shaping a world where education is not just a means of personal enrichment, but a collective effort to dismantle oppressive structures and create a more just and equitable society. In essence, it is a call to action, sparking a transformational movement to remove obstacles and achieve human flourishing. It is a call to individuals and communities to embrace the uncharted territories of possibility, reject imposed limitations, and collectively strive for a future in which the potential for human growth and liberation knows no bounds.

In the arduous task of reinventing ourselves, we need to delve deeply into the places where life escapes restriction, expands, and engages in a never-ending process of reinventing oneself. Thus, we need to transform ourselves from noisy and shallow streams into deep-water rivers, so that we

---

26. Freire, *Pedagogy of Hope*, 182.

can make expansive versions of ourselves. We need to challenge the stagnation of our waters—imposed by inflexible systems—and let these waters germinate fruitful and innovative ideas. Just like a river that is constantly moving, we also need to embrace the movement of our lives. Water without movement stagnates and rots. When motionless, it has no life. A river does not stop being a river because it converges with others, on the contrary, the confluence of rivers is a force that adds, increases and expands. We also cannot think that the movement of the waters of our lives, our emotions, prevent us from meeting other people and their emotions. We must think that meeting others has the potential to broaden and expand us. Our duty, as critical educators, lies not in solitary efforts, but in seamlessly integrating our efforts into a collective movement for emancipation, justice, and democracy, participating in the ongoing process of redesigning educational landscapes to embrace the complex knitted threads of our existence.

The realization that our work as educators cannot unfold in isolation underscores the interconnectedness of our efforts and how they are linked to our yearning for a greater cosmic connection. By recognizing ourselves as imaginative beings, we are called to harness the power of our creativity not only to forge innovative survival strategies, but, more importantly, to build new paradigms of *convivência* with other humans and more-than-humans. Our imaginative faculties will have to become instruments for sculpting inclusive educational environments, where diversity is celebrated, and differences are seen as assets rather than obstacles. In this way, creativity becomes a pillar in building a more comprehensive and interconnected society. Embracing a collective ethos, we align our efforts with the broader struggle for emancipation. By leveraging our imaginative capacities, we contribute to our personal evolution and the reformulation of social structures, promoting new inclusive forms of coexistence that transcend past limitations.

On our journey through life, we flow as tributaries on the river of life, welcoming the confluence of knowledge, traditions, cultures, and art, including the art of conviviality. By bathing in the richness of ancestral knowledge, we prepare ourselves for what is taking shape and evolving within and around us. And for this movement to flow, schools need to be critical, liberating, and loving. That's why we need to value the quality of connections, concerned not only with teaching people to become experts, but concerned with educating them to become happier, autonomous, and liberated. When school also becomes a place of *care with* and *care for* others, without distinction of gender, race, class, sexual orientation or age, we will have an excellent opportunity to heal our relationships. A pedagogy of tenderness will undoubtedly provide new synapses in our brains, resulting in a less complicated, sometimes avoided, brain process of showing and receiving affection.

Although a pedagogy of *convivência* may seem unattainable, we can educate ourselves for planetary *convivência*. I believe that an education intrinsically linked to the ethics of care, the demonstration of solidarity, and the exchange of affection is part of the praxis we need to achieve the untested feasibility. Remaining in a process of individualism and violence, neglect and indifference, will make us unviable as human beings and as a planet. Tenderness is vital to our existence and should be part of our pedagogical interactions. It is an essential element within the structure of the pedagogy of *convivência*. We need, then, to be literate in the cartography of affections. The dimension of affection, the reasons of the heart or the rights of the heart must be part of the conception of the pedagogy of *convivência*. Thinking of a pedagogy of *convivência* is impossible without thinking about attitudes of respect and reverence, and without equipping ourselves with attitudes of tenderness and affection. Displays of affection don't diminish us or make us less professional. A lack of affection diminishes us as people, making us bitter and insecure. To return our affection is to be able to show it, and thus to be able to do so will bring us benefits, not only for the people with whom we live, but for ourselves.

After all, even if the waters that overflow from the river of pragmatism try to invade the territories of humanity, whether in education or culture, by drowning the delicate plants that we cultivate there with affection and care, we can stubbornly imagine a pedagogy otherwise. Ultimately, in imagining a pedagogy of planetary *convivência*, may we become rivers of affection and our words become welcoming poetry, advancing against the turbulence of the murky waters of violence and indifference. In the circularity of our embraces, may we be able to set our affections in motion and thus travel through other territories. May we overflow through valleys and hills without losing the flux of the *Rio Grande* until we flow into the ocean of plentiful *convivência*.

Bibliography

Abel, Emily K., and Margaret Nelson, eds. *Circles of Care*. Albany: SUNY Press, 1990.
Abdi, Ali A. and Paul R. Carr (eds.). *Educating for Democratic Consciousness: Counter-hegemonic Possibilities*. New York: Lang, 2013.
Abu Toha, Mosab. *Things You Might Find Hidden in My Ear: Poems from Gaza*. San Francisco: City Lights, 2022.
Acosta, Alberto. *O Bem Viver—Uma Oportunidade para Imaginar outros mundos*. Elefante. Kindle Edition.
Adichie, Chimamanda Ngozi. "The Danger of a Single Story." TED Conferences LLC, July 2009, www.ted.com/talks/chimamanda_adichie_the_danger_of_a_single_story.
Alexander, M. Jacqui. *Pedagogies of Crossing: Meditations on Feminism, Sexual Politics, Memory, and the Sacred*. Durham: Duke University Press, 2005.
Alves, Rubem. *A Alegria de Ensinar*. São Paulo: Ars Poetica, 1994.
———. *Conversas com Quem Gosta de Ensinar—Sobre Jequitibás e Eucaliptos (Conversations with those who Like to Teach—About Sycamor and Eucalyptus)*. São Paulo: Cortez, 1983.
———. *A Escola com que Sempre Sonhei sem Imaginar que Pudesse Existir*. São Paulo: Papirus, 2012.
Anzaldúa, Gloria. *Borderlands/La Frontera: The New Mestiza*. 3rd ed. San Francisco: Aunt Lute, 2007.
Arendt, Hannah. *The Human Condition*. Chicago: University of Chicago Press. 1969.
Assmann, Hugo and Franz Hinkelammert. *A Idolatria do Mercado: Ensaio sobre Economia e Teologia*. São Paulo: Vozes, 1989.
Baker-Fletcher, Karen. *Sisters of Dust, Sisters of Spirit: Womanist Wordings on God and Creation*. Minneapolis: Fortress, 1998.
Bauman, Zygmunt. *Community: Seeking Safety in an Insecure World*. Cambridge: Polity, 2001.
———. *Modernidade Líquida*. Rio de Janeiro: Zahar, 2001.
bell hooks. *Feminism Is for Everybody: Passionate Politics*. Cambridge, MA: South End, 2000.
———. *Feminist Theory from Margin to Center*. Boston: South End, 1984.
———. *Teaching to Transgress: Education as the Practice of Freedom*. New York: Routledge, 1994.

Bibliography

Boff, Leonardo. *O Cuidado Necessário: Na Vida, na saúde, na educação, na ecologia, na ética e na espiritualidade.* Petrópolis, RJ: Vozes, 2012.

———. *O Despertar da Aguia: O dia-bólico e o sim-bólico na construção da realidade.* Petrópolis, RJ: Vozes, 1998.

———. *Los derechos del corazón: El rescate de la inteligencia cordial.* Mexico: Dabar, 2015, Kindle Edition.

———. *Ecologia Humana: Una Estrategia de Intervención Cultural.* Santafe de Bogotá: San Pablo, 1997.

———. *Ecology & Liberation: A New Paradigm.* Ecology and Justice Series. Maryknoll, NY: Orbis, 1995.

———. *Essential Care: An Ethics of Human Nature.* Waco, TX: Baylor University Press, 2008.

———. *Global Civilization: Challenges to Society and Christianity.* London: Equinox, 2005.

———. *Nova Era: A Civilização Planetária.* São Paulo: Ática, 1995.

———. *Princípio de Compaixão e Cuidado.* Petrópolis, RJ: Vozes, 2000.

———. *Princípio-Terra: A Volta À Terra Como Pátria Comum.* São Paulo: Ática, 1994.

———. *Saber Cuidar: ética do humano, compaixão pela terra.* São Paulo: Vozes, 17a. ed, 2011.

———. *Virtues: For Another Possible World.* Eugene, OR: Cascade Books, 2011.

Bonin, Iara. "O Bem Viver Indígena e o futuro da humanidade." *Encarte Pedagógico* X (2016) 1–4. https://www.cimi.org.br/pub/Porantim/2015/Encarte_Porantim381_dez2016.pdf.

Bristol, Laurette. *Plantation Pedagogy: Postcolonial and Global Perspective.* New York: Lang, 2012.

Brown, Wendy. *Undoing the Demos: Neoliberalism's Stealth Revolution.* New York: Zone, 2015.

Brueggemann, Walter. *Interrupting Silence: God's Command to Speak Out.* Louisville: Westminster John Knox, 2018.

———. *The Prophetic Imagination.* 2nd ed. Minneapolis: Fortress, 2001.

Burrow, Rufus, Jr. *Ethical Prophets along the Way: Those Hall of Famers.* Eugene, OR: Cascade Books, 2020.

Butler, Judith. *Precarious Life: The Power of Mourning and Violence.* London: Verso, 2004.

———. "Vida Precária." Translation by Angelo Macedo Vasco. *Contemporânea: Dossiê Diferenças e (Des)Igualdades* 1 (2011) 13–33.

Case, Kim, ed. *Intersectional Pedagogy: Complicating Identity and Social Justice.* New York: Routledge, 2017.

Chatzidakis, Andreas, et al. *The Care Manifesto: The Politics of Independence.* London: Verso, 2020.

Chomsky, Noam. *Chomsky on Miseducation.* Introduced and edited by Donaldo Macedo. Critical Perspectives Series. Lanham, MD: Rowman & Littlefield, 2000.

Convivialist Manifesto: A Declaration of Interdependence. Global Dialogues 3 (2014). M. Clarke, trans. https://doi.org/10.14282/2198-0403-GD-3.

Cortella, Mario Sergio. *Educação Convivência e Ética: Audácia e Esperança!* São Paulo: Cortez, 2015.

Cully, Iris V., and Kendig Brubaker Cully, eds. *Harper's Encyclopedia of Religious Education.* San Francisco: Harper & Row, 1990.

Darder, Antonia. *Freire and Education.* New York: Routledge, 2015.

Bibliography

———. *The Student Guide to Freire's "Pedagogy of the Oppressed."* London: Bloomsbury, 2018.

Darder, Antonia et al., eds. *International Critical Pedagogy Reader*. 2nd ed. New York: Routledge, 2016.

Daymia, Vrinda. "Vulnerability, Precarity, and the Ambivalent Interventions of Emphatic Care." In *Care Ethics in the Age of Precarity*, 68–90. Minneapolis: University of Minnesota Press, 2021.

Democracy Now! "Palestinian Poet Mosab Abu Toha Decries Israel's 'Inhumane' Assault as Gaza Death Toll Tops 25,000." Transcript of interview of Palestinian poet Mosab Abu Toha by Amy Goodman, January 22, 2024. https://www.democracynow.org/2024/1/22/mosab_abu_toha_gaza/.

Dussel, Enrique. *Ethics of Liberation in the Age of Globalization and Exclusion*. Latin America Otherwise. Durham: Duke University Press, 2013.

———. *1492 El Encubrimiento del Otro: Hacia el Origen del "Mito de la Modernidad."* La Paz: Plural, 1994.

Fals Borda, Orlando. *Una sociología sentipensante para América Latina*. Bogota: Siglo del Hombre/CLACSO, 2009.

Fanon, Frantz. *The Wretched of the Earth*. Translated by Constance Farrington. New York: Grove, 1963.

Francis, Pope. *Laudato Si': Sobre o Cuidado da Casa Comum*. São Paulo: Paulus/Loyola, 2015.

Friedman, Marilyn, ed. *Women and Citizenship*. New York: Oxford University Press, 2005.

Freire, Ana Maria Araújo. *Paulo Freire: Uma História de Vida*. São Paulo: Paz e Terra, 2017.

Freire, Ana Maria Araújo (org.). *A Pedagogia da Libertação em Paulo Freire*. São Paulo: Editora UNESP, 1999.

———. (org.) *Paulo Freire: Pedagogia dos Sonhos Possíveis*. São Paulo: UNESP, 2001.

———. (org.) *Cartas a Cristina: Reflexões sobre minha vida e minha práxis*. São Paulo: Paz e Terra, 2013.

———. (org.) *Pedagogia da Tolerância*. São Paulo: Paz e Terra, 2014.

———. (org.) *Testamento da Presença de Paulo Freire, o Educador do Brasil: Testemunhos e Depoimentos*. São Paulo: Paz e Terra, 2021.

———. (org.) *Boniteza: A Palavra Boniteza na Leitura de Mundo de Paulo Freire*. São Paulo: Paz e Terra, 2022.

Freire, Paulo. *Educação como Prática da Liberdade*. 40ª ed. Rio de Janeiro: Paz & Terra, 1965/2017.

———. *A Letter to a Theology Student*. Washington, DC: LADOC, 1972. v. II.

———. *Pedagogia da Esperança: Um Reencontro com a Pedagogia do Oprimido*. São Paulo: Paz e Terra, 1992.

———. *Pedagogy of Commitment: Paulo Freire*. Boulder: Paradigm Publishers, 2014. Paz e Terra, 1994.

———. *Pedagogy of Freedom: Ethics, Democracy, and Civic Courage*. New York: Rowman & Littlefield, 2001.

———. *Pedagogy of the Heart*. New York: Continuum, 1998.

———. *Pedagogy of Hope: Reliving Pedagogy of the Oppressed*. New York: Continuum, 2007.

———. *Pedagogy of Indignation*. Boulder, CO: Paradigm, 2004.

Bibliography

———. *The Pedagogy of the Oppressed.* 20th Anniversary ed. New York: Continuum, 1997.

———. *Pedagogy of Solidarity.* Walnut Creek, CA: Left Coast, 2014.

———. *Pedagogia da Tolerância.* 3. ed., Rio de Janeiro/ São Paulo: Paz & Terra, 2014.

———. *Política e Educação, 8ª. ed.,* São Paulo: Villa das Letras, 1997.

———. *The Politics of Education: Culture Power and Liberation.* Massachusetts: Bergin & Garvey, 1985.

———. *The Politics of Education.* Westport, CT.: Bergin & Garvey, 1995.

———. *Professora Sim, Tia Não: Cartas a Quem Ousa Ensinar.* São Paulo: Olho d'Agua, 1993.

———. *Teachers as Cultural Workers: Letters to Those Who Dare Teach.* The Edge, Critical Studies in Educational Theory. Boulder, CO: Westview, 1998.

Freire, Paulo, e Donaldo Macedo. *Alfabetização: leitura do mundo, leitura da palavra.* São Paulo: Paz e Terra, 2011.

Freire, Paulo, e Antonio Faundez. *Por uma pedagogia da pergunta.* 9th Ed. Rio de Janeiro: Paz e Terra, 2019.

Fu-Kiau, K. Kia B., and A. M. Lukondo-Wamba, *Kindezi: The Kongo Art of Babysitting.* Baltimore: INPRINT, 2000.

Gadotti, Moacir. *Pedagogy of Praxis: A Dialectical Philosophy of Education.* Albany: State University of New York Press, 1996.

Galeano, Eduardo. *The Book of Embraces.* New York: Norton 1992.

———. *Las Palabras Andantes.* Argentina: Catalogos. 1993.

———. *As Veias Abertas da América Latina,* trad. Galeno de Freitas, 23a ed. Rio de Janeiro: Paz e Terra, 1986.

Garrard, Virginia. "Hidden in Plain Sight: Dominion Theology, Spiritual Warfare, and Violence in Latin America" in *Religions* (2020) Vol. 11, Issue 2, 648.

Giroux, Henry. *Border Crossings: Cultural Workers and the Politics of Education.* New York: Routledge, 1992.

———. *Education and the Crisis of Public Values: Challenging the Assault on Teachers, Students, and Public Education.* New York: Lang, 2015.

———. *On Critical Pedagogy.* New York: Bloomsbury, 2013.

———. *Race, Politics, and Pandemic Pedagogy: Education in a Time of Crisis.* London: Bloomsbury Academic, 2021.

———. *Teachers as Intellectuals: Toward a Critical Pedagogy of Learning.* Westport, CT: Bergin &Garvey, 1988.

———. *The Violence of Organized Forgetting: Thinking Beyond America's Disimagination Machine.* San Francisco: City Lights Bookstore, 2014.

Grande, Sandy. *Red Pedagogy: Native American Social and Political Thought.* 10th Anniversary ed. New York: Rowman & Littlefield, 2015.

Greene, Maxine. *Releasing the Imagination: Essays on Education, the Arts, and Social Change.* San Francisco: Jossey-Bassey, 1995.

Gutierrez, Gustavo. *A Theology of Liberation.* Maryknoll, NY: Orbis, 1991.

Hamington, Maurice, and Michael Flower, eds. *Care Ethics in the Age of Precarity.* Minneapolis: University of Minnesota Press, 2021.

Hampson, Tom, and Loretta Whalen, *Tales of the Heart: Affective Approaches to Global Education.* Cincinnati: Friendship, 1991.

Heidegger, Martin. *Being and Time.* (Macquarrie & Robinson, trans.). Oxford: Blackwell, 1962.

Bibliography

———. *Ser e Tempo*, Parte I, Márcia de Sá Cavalcante (Trans.), Petrópolis, RJ: Vozes, 1989.
Held, Virginia. *The Ethics of Care: Personal, Political, and Global*. New York: Oxford University Press, 2006.
Herzog, William, II. *Parables as Subversive Speech: Jesus as Pedagogue of the Oppressed*. Louisville: Westminster John Knox, 1994.
Heschel, Abraham. *The Insecurity of Freedom: Essays on Human Existence*. New York: Farrar Straus & Giroux, 1966.
———. *The Prophets*. Vol. 2. New York: Harper & Row, 1962.
Hintzen-Bohlen, Brigitte. *Andalusia—Art and Architecture*. German: Ullmann, 2006.
Holquist, Michael. *Dialogism: Bakhtin and His World*. New York: Routledge, 1990.
Illich, Ivan. *Deschooling Society*. New York: Harper & Row, 1971.
———. *Tools for Conviviality*. New York: Harper & Row, 1973.
Irwin, Robert. *The Alhambra*. Cambridge: Harvard University Press, 2004.
Isasi-Diaz, Ada Maria, and Eduardo Mendieta. *Decolonizing Epistemologies: Latina/o Theologyand Philosophy*. New York: Fordham University Press, 2012.
Kim, Grace Ji-Sun, and Jann Aldredge-Clanton, eds. *Intercultural Ministry: Hope for a Changing World*. Valley Forge, PA: Judson, 2017.
Kim, Grace Ji-Sun, and Hilda P. Koster, eds. *Planetary Solidarity: Global Women's Voices on Christian Doctrine and Climate Justice*. Minneapolis: Fortress, 2017.
King, Martin Luther, Jr. *Why We Can't Wait*. New York: Signet, 2000.
King, Ursula. *The Search for Spirituality: Our Global Quest for a Spiritual Life*. Katonah, NY: Blue Bridge, 2008.
Kirylo, James. *Paulo Freire: The Man from Recife*. New York: Bloomsbury, 2020.
Kirylo, James, and Drick Boyd, *Paulo Freire: His Faith, Spirituality, and Theology*. Rotterdam: Sense, 2017.
Kirylo, James, ed. *Reinventing "Pedagogy of the Oppressed."* New York: Bloomsbury, 2020.
Kozulin, Alex, et al. *Vygotsky's Educational Theory in Cultural Context*. Cambridge: Cambridge University Press, 2003.
Krenak, Ailton. *A Vida Não é Útil*. (*Life is Not Useful*). São Paulo: Companhia das Letras, 2020.
———. *Futuro Ancestral*. São Paulo: Companhia das Letras. 2022.
———. *Ideias para Adiar o Fim do Mundo*. São Paulo: Companhia das Letras. 2019.
Krenak, Ailton, e Yussef Campos. *Lugares de Origem*. São Paulo: Jandaíra. 2021.
Libaneo, José Carlos. *Pedagogia e Pedagogos, Para Quê?* São Paulo: Cortez, 2002.
Lovat, Terence John, and Robert Crotty. *Reconciling Islam, Christianity and Judaism: Islam's Special Role in Restoring Convivencia*. New York: Springer, 2015.
Mann, Vivian, et al., eds. *Convivencia: Jews, Muslims, and Christians in Medieval Spain*. New York: Braziller, 2007.
Maturama, Humberto. *Transformación en la Convivencia*. Buenos Aires: Granica, 2014.
Maturama, Humberto, and Francisco Varela. *The Tree of Knowledge: The Biological Roots of Human Understanding*. Boston: Shambhala, 1998.
Mbembe, Achille. *Necropolitics*. Durham: Duke University Press, 2019.
McLaren, Peter. *Critical Pedagogy and Predatory Culture: Oppositional Politics in a Postmodern Era*. New York: Routledge, 1995.
McLaren, Peter, and Peter Leonard. *Paulo Freire: A Critical Encounter*. London: Routledge, 1993.

Bibliography

McLaren, Peter, and Colin Lankshear. *Politics of Liberation: Paths from Freire*. New York: Routledge, 1994.

McLaren, Peter, and Petar Jandric. *Post-Digital Dialogues on Critical Pedagogy, Liberation Theology and Information Technology*. New York: Bloomsbury, 2020.

Medrut, Flavia, comp. "Inspirational Quotes from Malcolm X on Life, Education Freedom and the Media." https://www.goalcast.com/malcolm-x-quotes/. Accessed October 3, 2018.

Memmi, Albert. *The Colonizer and the Colonized*. Boston: Beacon, 1967.

Mohanty, Chandra Talpade. *Feminism without Borders*. Durham: Duke University Press, 2003.

Noddings, Nel. *Educating Moral People: A Caring Alternative to Character Education*. New York: Teachers College, Columbia University, 2002.

———. *Caring: A Relational Approach to Ethics & Moral Education*. Los Angeles: University of California Press, 2013.

———, ed. *Educating Citizens for Global Awareness. A Relational Approach to Ethics & Moral Education*. New York: Teachers College, Columbia University, 2005.

Nussbaum, Martha. *Not for Profit*. Princeton: Princeton University Press, 2010.

Palmer, Parker. *The Courage to Teach: Exploring the Inner Landscape of Teacher's Life*. San Francisco: Jossey-Bass, 1998.

———. *Healing the Heart of Democracy: The Courage to Create a Politics Worthy of the Human Spirit*. San Francisco: Jossey-Bass, 2011.

———. *To Know as We Are Known: Education as a Spiritual Journey*. 1st HarperCollins San Francisco: Harper San Francisco, 1993.

Povinelli, Elizabeth A. Povinelli, "The Will to Be Otherwise/ The Effort of Endurance" *South Atlantic Quarterly* (2012) 111 (3): 453–75.

Ray, Siladitya. "'No Electricity, No Food, No Fuel': Israel Orders 'Complete Siege' on Gaza Strip." *Forbes*, October 9, 2023. https://www.forbes.com/sites/siladityaray/2023/10/09/no-electricity-no-food-no-fuel-israel-orders-complete-siege-on-gaza-strip/?sh=13a0515060c8/.

Restrepo, Luis Carlos. *El Derecho a la Ternura*. Bogotá: Arango Editores, 1st Ed. 1994.

———. *Ecologia Humana: Una Estrategia de Intervención Cultural*. Santafe de Bogotá: San Pablo, 1997.

Ribeiro, Sidarta. *Sonho Manifesto: Dez exercícios urgentes de otimismo apocalíptico*. São Paulo: Companhia Das Letras, 2022.

Rodriguez, Clelia O. *Decolonizing Academia: Poverty, Oppression, and Pain*, Nova Scotia: Fernwood, 2018.

Rose-Redwood, Rueben, et al. "Decolonizing the Map: Recentering Indigenous Mappings," *Cartographica* 55 (2020), 151–62.

Santos, Boaventura de Sousa. *Descolonizar el saber, Reinventar el poder*. Uruguai: Trilce, 2010.

———. *The End of the Cognitive Empire: The Coming of Age of Epistemologies of the South*. Durham: Duke University Press. 2018.

———. *Epistemologies of the Global South. Justice Against Epistemicide*. New York: Routledge, 2014.

Santos, Boaventura de Sousa and Maria Paula Meneses, eds. *Knowledges Born in the Struggle: Constructing the Epistemologies of the Global South*. New York: Routledge, 2020.

Bibliography

Schlein, Lisa. "WHO: Gaza Cut Off from Food, Water, 'Anything Which Is Necessary for Any Sort of Life.'" VOA News (website), December 8, 2023. https://www.voanews.com/a/who-gaza-cut-off-from-food-water-anything-which-is-necessary-for-any-sort-of-life-/7390360.html/.

Schüssler Fiorenza, Elisabeth. *Democratizing Biblical Studies: Toward an Emancipatory Educational Space*. Louisville: Westminster John Knox, 2009.

———. *Searching the Scriptures: A Feminist Commentary*. New York: Crossroad Herder, 1998.

"The Second Convivialist Manifesto: Towards a Post-Neoliberal World." *Civic Sociology*, (2020) June.

Segato, Rita. *Contra-pedagogías de la crueldad*. Ciudad Autónoma de Buenos Aires: Prometeo, 2018.

Seymour, Jack. *Teaching the Way of Jesus: Educating Christians for Faithful Living*. Nashville: Abingdon, 2014.

Simpson, Leanne Betasamosake. *As We Have Always Done: Indigenous Freedom through Radical Resistance*. Minneapolis: University of Minnesota Press, 1917.

Sorrells, Kathryn. *Intercultural Communication: Globalization and Social Justice*. 3rd ed. Thousand Oaks, CA: Sage, 2022.

Sinner, Rudolf von. *Confiança e Convivência: Reflexões Éticas e Ecumênicas*. São Leopoldo, RS: Sinodal, 2007.

Souto-Manning, Mariana. *Freire, Teaching, and Learning: Culture Circles across Contexts*. New York: Lang, 2010.

Suess, Paulo. *Elementos para a busca do Bem Viver (Sumak Kawsay) para todos e sempre*. 2010. https://cimi.org.br/2010/12/elementos-para-a-busca-do-bem-viver-sumak-kawsay-para-todos-e-sempre/.

Takuá, Kristina. *Rebento* (São Paulo) 9 (2018) 5–8.

Tronto, Joan. *Caring Democracy: Markets, Equality, and Justice*. New York: Lang, 2011.

Tronto, Joan, and Berenice Fisher. "Toward a Feminist Theory of Caring." In *Circles of Care*, edited by Emily K. Abel and Margaret Nelson, 36–54. Albany: State University of New York Press, 1990.

Turner, Victor. *The Ritual Process. Structure and Anti-structure*. New York: Aldine de Gruyter, 1995.

Tutu, Desmond. *God Is Not a Christian—And Other Provocations*. Edited by John Allen. New York: HarperOne, 2011.

Vizenor, Gerald. *Manifest Manners: Narratives on Postindian Survivance*. Lincoln: University of Nebraska Press, 1999.

Volf, Miroslav. *A Public Faith: How Followers of Christ Should Serve the Common Good*. Grand Rapids: Brazos, 2011.

Walsh, Catherine, ed. *Pedagogias Decoloniales. Praticas Insurgentes de resistir, (re) existir y (re) vivir*. Tomo I. Quito: Abyayala, 2013.

Wilde, Sandra. *Care in Education: Teaching with Understanding and Compassion*. New York: Routledge, 2013.

Zinn, Howard, and Donaldo Macedo. *Howard Zinn on Democratic Education*. Boulder, CO: Paradigm, 2005.

Index

adaptation, 100
Adichie, Chimamanda Ngozi, 140
affection, 137, 138, 144. *See also* cartography of affection
Alexander, Jacqui, 26
Alhambra Palace (Granada), 32
"Aloha," 8
Alves, Rubem, 94–95
anthropocentrism, 12
Anzaldua, Gloria, 7
archaeology, 129–31
Argentina, 8
artificial intelligence, 92
assessment, 68
Assmann, Hugo, 57
atravessada (crossed), 7–8, 9
attentiveness, 73
authoritarianism, 51
Ayamara people, 41
Aztecs, 20

Baker-Fletcher, Karen, 17
Bakhtin, Mikhail, 3
banking model of education, 59, 62–63, 133
Bauman, Zygmunt, 30
becoming concept, 99
"being more," 64
biophilia, 57–58
body, as political territory, 133
Boff, Leonardo
    on the Aztecs, 20
    on coexistence, 38, 43
    on dimension of care, 81–82, 84, 85
    on fundamentalism, 52
    on good Samaritan parable, 89–90
    on the heart, 19
    on Heidegger, 83
    on oppression and exclusion, 57
Bolivia, 43
Borda, Orlando Fals, 134
borderland identity, 7
brain, 138
Brazil, ethnicities in, 39n22
Brown, Wendy, 56, 59
buen vivir (good living/living well), 11–12, 41–42, 43
Butler, Judith, 74

Cabral, Amilcar, 21n19
Caillé, Alain, 34
Camara, Dom Hélder, 81n14
Campos, Márcio, 108
capitalism, 18, 23, 58, 102
care
    as attitude, 83
    The Care Manifesto, 79–81
    collaboration for, 80
    in democratic political life, 75
    devaluing, 71–72
    development of, 72
    distribution of, 74
    of the earth, 76–77, 81–82
    in education, 77–79, 85
    empathetic, 72, 78
    as ethical responsibility, 81

Index

care (*cont.*)
    fable of, 83
    feminist care theory and, 75
    as fundamental, 72
    importance of, 12–13, 69–70
    incorporation of, 92
    intelligence for, 72–73
    lack of, 70
    in Latin American liberation theology, 89
    need for, 71–77
    neglect *versus,* 83
    ontological aspect of, 73
    overview of, 70–71
    politicization of, 72
    reimagining of, 73, 74
    relational and cooperative aspects of, 76
    in relationships, 73, 82
    spiritual perspective of, 13, 81–85
    taking care of each other with, 85–90
    value of, 36
    as way of being, 83–84
The Care Manifesto, 79–81
care-full education, 13
cartography of affection
    archaeologizing of emotions in, 130–31
    as bridge, 134
    embracing, in education, 134–35
    as guide, 135
    mapping of inner landscape in, 127–30
    navigation with, 136
    overview of, 131–44
    social transformation through, 136
Chancoso, Blanca, 41
Chatzidakis, Andreas, 79
Christians, failures of, 44
citizenship, 56, 59, 62, 65–67
civic illiteracy, 62
coexistence, 28, 30, 46, 91, 92–93
cognitive extractivism, 37
cognitive justice, 37
collaboration, 80, 128–29
collective resistance, 140
colonial pedagogy, 141
colonialism, 3, 4, 23, 24, 109
colonization, 15, 65
communication, 21
community, 2, 3, 6, 28, 79
companions, 25
companionship, 25
company, 25
compassion, 78, 89–90
conscientization, 4, 22, 53, 60, 64–65, 113n30
consciousness, 3, 60
consumerism, 19–20, 35, 58
convivência (conviviality)
    ancestral understanding of, 39–49
    challenges of, 29, 30–31
    coexistence and, 30
    decline of, 30
    defined, 11, 28, 30, 31–32n5, 38, 48
    deliberate approach for, 45–46
    diligence in, 31
    examples of, 32
    as fostered, 136
    historical context of, 31–33
    intentionality in, 31
    key ideas on nature of tool of, 33–34
    as learning process, 136
    overview of, 24, 25
    path to, 29
    political dimension of, 33
    promotion of, 45
    recognition of presence and value of others in, 112–13
    social dimension of, 33
Convivialist Manifesto, 34–37
corazonar (to warm up the heart), 17, 19
coronavirus pandemic, 19, 44–45, 73, 97
Correa, Rafael, 43
cosmos, 128
cosmovision, 41–42
creativity, 143
Crenshaw, Kimberlé, 53n5
critical consciousness, 134
critical education, function of, 12. *See also* education
critical mindset, 65
critical thinking, 22
crossing borders, 7, 8
cultural-historical activity theory (CHAT), 60n19

Index

culture of cruelty, 101–2

Dalmya, Vrinda, 72
Darder, Antonia, 17, 114, 133
decolonial approaches, in religious education, 4
decolonial mapping, 132
dedication, 73
dehumanization, 63–64, 109, 110, 118
democracy, 12, 50, 52, 56, 59, 60, 75
des-norteada (person without north), 108
destruction, 100
diabolical *(diaballein)*, 38
dialogical action, 121
dialogical approach to education, 119–22
dialogue, 51, 54, 64, 119–22, 141
dignity, 53
dominion theology, 51
dreams, 128
Dussel, Enrique, 57, 109, 140

earth
    capitalism and, 102
    care for, 76–77, 81–82
    destruction to, 102–3
    engagement with problems of, 118–19
    humanity's relationship with, 103
    as shared home, 122
    spiritual connection with, 9–10
economic religion, 57
ecosystem, degradation of, 70
Ecuador, 43
education
    accountability in, 62
    as assembly line, 58–59
    assessment in, 68
    banking model of, 59, 62–63, 133
    care in, 77–79, 85
    The Care Manifesto for, 79–81
    care-full, 91–93
    central role of, 4–5, 6
    challenges in, 16
    characteristics of, 144
    citizenship, 65–67
    co-investigation in, 62
    collaboration in, 21, 128–29
    colonization impact on, 15, 65
    conscientization and, 53
    corporate world aspects in, 61–62
    as critical and emancipatory, 67
    as designed by dominant class, 22
    dialogical approach to, 119–22
    dialogue in, 54
    dimensions of, 12
    diverse perspectives in, 55
    emancipatory, 5, 52–53
    empowerment in, 66
    equipping in, 66–67
    establishment, 4
    failures of, 18, 24
    focus in, 16
    for-profit, 61, 62
    of the heart, 16, 18, 19, 20
    higher, 59
    historical changes in, 34
    history textbooks in, 55
    of hope, 111–12
    individualism in, 129
    interconnectedness in, 143
    learning space description in, 55
    liberation pedagogy for, 63–64
    as mechanical, 13
    neoliberalism and, 58–59, 60, 63
    pedagogy of lies in, 55
    as practice of freedom, 109, 110
    relationships in, 78
    religious, 2–3, 4, 22
    resistance and, 67
    role of, 54
    sense of agency in, 66
    shaping impact in, 67
    social interaction role of, 5
    social responsibility in, 54, 61, 67–68
    social structures and, 59
    societal norm reproduction in, 55
    teacher-learner contradiction in, 62
    training *versus*, 60n20
    transformation in, 13, 21, 67, 68
    utopian dimension of, 106–7
    See also specific types
educators
    courage of, 126
    emotional skills of, 126
    interconnectedness of, 143
    lovingness of, 117, 118, 119
    solidarity of, 123, 124

Index

educators (*cont.*)
    teachers as compared to, 94–95
    See also teachers
emancipatory education, 5. *See also* education
emotional intelligence, 84
emotions
    as absent in education process, 16–17
    appreciation for, 135–36
    archaeologizing of, 130–31
    awareness of, 135
    as dynamic force, 14
    embracing, 140
    exploration of, 135–36
    illiteracy of, 139
    mapping, 134–35
    pain in, 129–30
    reaction to, 129
    reason and, 17
    terrains of, 136
    visibility and tangibility of, 134
    See also cartography of affection
empathy, 23, 55, 72, 78, 136
environment, 102
establishment education, 4. *See also* education
ethics of solidarity, 63, 124–25
eucalyptus trees, 95
exclusion, 57
existing, 99–100
experience, diversity of, 4
exploitation, of nature, 43

fanaticism, 51, 52
Fanon, Frantz, 21, 65
Federal University of Minas Gerais (UFMG), 29n3
feminist care theory, 75
Fisher, Berenice, 72
Francis (Pope), 76
Freire, Anna Maria Araujo, 108
Freire, Nita, 64, 100, 108, 129
Freire, Paulo
    on "being more," 64
    on body, 133
    on collectivity, 142
    on colonialism, 109
    on communication, 21
    on conscientization, 22, 60
    on critical consciousness, 134
    on critical thinking, 22
    decolonialism of, 21
    on democracy, 60
    on dialogue, 119–22
    on economy, 57–58
    on education, 4–5, 53n5, 54, 59, 62–63
    as educator, 109
    on emotion, 129
    as epistemologist, 133
    ethical work of, 21–22
    on existence, 100
    on generative words, 13
    on heart, 20
    on history, 50
    on hope, 70, 110–14
    influence of, 6–7, 15
    on interaction, 21
    legacy of, 114
    on liberation pedagogy, 63–64
    on literacy, 13
    on lovingness, 114–19
    on neoliberal ideology, 63
    overview of, 15n1
    on personhood, 64
    on praxis, 24n22
    on solidarity, 122–26
    sulear and, 108–10
    on transformation, 16
Fu-Kiau, K. Kia B., 91
fundamentalism, 50, 51, 52
The Fundamentals, 52

Galeano, Eduardo, 27, 29, 133–34
Garrard, Virginia, 51–52
generative words, 13
Giroux, Henry, 26, 54, 62, 65–66, 101, 103
global economy, 60
global relationships, 3
globalization, 15, 24
God, love of, 84–85
golden rule, 86
Good Samaritan, 85–90
Greene, Maxime, 95
greetings, 48
Guarani people, 8, 39–40, 42, 46
Gutierrez, Gustavo, 57, 89

Index

heart
    centrality of, 18–19, 20, 21
    complexities of, 135
    education of, 16, 18, 19, 20
    function of, 18
    growth of, 17
    hope and care from, 19
    mind unity with, 20–21
    rigidity of, 20
    significance of, 20
Heck, Egon, 42
Heidegger, Martin, 82–83
Held, Virginia, 79
herida abierta (open wound), 7
Herzog, William, 86
Heschel, Abraham Joshua, 18, 69, 73, 84–85
Hicotea Man, 134
higher education, 59
Hinkelammert, Franz, 57
historical-methodological approach, 60n19
history education, 55
homo oeconomicus, 56, 57
hope, 70, 110–14, 140–41
horizon, 41
horizontalization, 126
hugging, 9
human connections, 38, 39, 44, 47, 48
human rights, 53
humanity
    adaptation by, 100
    archaeological exercises of, 130
    becoming by, 99
    deterioration of, 103
    dialogue among, 119–22
    educability of, 99
    as existing, 99–100
    as fellow travelers, 128
    as *Homo sapiens aggressans*, 137
    as *homo sapiens amans*, 137
    marking and shaping of, 106
    mind and heart connection in, 107
    reinvention by, 100
    relationship with earth by, 103
    shared principles of, 22–23
    solidarity among, 122–26
    subjectivity of, 119–20
humanization, *amorosidade* in praxis of, 117–18
Humbert, Marc, 34

idolatry, 57
ignorance, 62
II International Conference on Environmental Education, 27–28
Illich, Ivan, 33–34
immune system, 138
Indigenous peoples, 132
individualism, 35, 43–44, 48, 122, 129
industrial society, 33–34
injunction, 98
injustices, 59
inner landscape, mapping of, 127–30
insularity, 47
intellectual intelligence, 84
intelligence, 72–73, 137
interconnectedness, 22, 23
Intercultural Formation for Indigenous Educators (FIEI) degree, 29
intercultural immersion, 3
interdependence, 4
international communication, 24
International Journal "Cartographica," 132
intersectionality, 53n5
intolerance, 51
intransigence, 51
intuition, 16
isolation, 3, 112

Jesus Christ, 44, 45, 85–90
Jews, 87

Kia Ora, 8–9
Kindezi, 91
kindness, 48
King, Martin Luther, Jr., 47–48, 81n14, 101, 131
knowledge, 3, 16, 17, 37, 60, 60n19
Kongo, 91
Krenak, Ailton, 104, 127, 131

land, 9–10, 42. *See also* earth
language, elimination of, 29–30
Latin America, Pentecostalism in, 51

Index

Latin American liberation theology, 89
Latouche, Serge, 34
Lévinas, Emmanuel, 20
liberation pedagogy, 63–64, 107, 133
lifestyle alternatives, 44
liminality, 98–99
limit-situations, 22, 142
localism, 36
Loebens, Francisco, 42
love, 137–38
love of God, 84–85
lovingness (amorosidade), 114–19, 141
Lukondo-Wamba, A. M., 91

Macedo, Donaldo, 55, 129
Machado, Antonio, 127
mapping, 132
marginalization, 61
Márquez, Gabriel Garcia, 15
material possessions, idolizing, 57
Maturana, Humberto, 137
Mbembe, Achille, 58
Memmi, Albert, 21, 65
memory, 41
mental processes, emphasis on, 128
mestiza consciousness, 7
metanoia, 47
mind, heart unity with, 20–21
Mohanty, Chandra, 61
movements, river analogy and, 106
mutuality, 131

Nahuatl people, 20
National Plan for Good Living, 43
natural disasters, 102
nature, 38, 43, 106. *See also* earth
necrophilia, 57–58
necropolitics, 58
neglect, 83
neoliberal project, 58
neoliberal system, 18, 43
neoliberalism, 35, 36, 56, 58–59, 60, 63
Nishnaabeg, Michi Saagiig, 37
Noddings, Nell, 78
nortear (orient or guide), 108
nurturing, 36
Nussbaum, Martha, 60–61

oppression, 57–58, 65
Other, 74
otherness, 4, 8, 44
outwardness, 4

Pachamama (Mother Earth), 9, 40
pain, 129–30
Palmer, Parker, 16, 18–19, 96
pandemics, characteristics of, 97. *See also* coronavirus pandemic
parable of the Good Samaritan, 85–90
paradigmatic changes, characteristics of, 96–97
pathos, 84
patriarchy, 23
Paul (apostle), 17
pedagogy, 25–26, 91, 141. *See also* education
Pedagogy of Hope (Freire), 110
pedagogy of lies, 55
Pentecostals, 51
personhood, 64
Pessoa, Fernando, 94
planetary community, rupture and chaos in, 97
planetary vision, 23
plurality, 51
politics, 52
politics of humiliation, 101
poverty, 58
Povinelli, Elizabeth, 70
power dynamics, 53
praxis, 24n22
precarity, 74
profits, pursuit of, 102
Prosperity Gospel movement, 58

Qonakuy, 8
Quéchua people, 41

racism, 23
radical coexistence, 29–30
re-aggregation, 98
reason, 17
reinvention, 100
relationships, 3, 73, 78, 82
religion, 52, 57, 58
religious communities, 23

Index

religious education, 2–3, 4, 22. *See also* education
religious extremism, 33
religious formation, 2
religious fundamentalism, 51
religious intolerance, 52
resilience, 140
resistance, 8, 67
resource shortages, 102
respect, 48, 122
Restrepo, Luis Carlos, 138–39
Ribeiro, Sidarta, 19
Rilke, Rainer Maria, 1
Rio Grande de La Magdelena, 134
rivers/river metaphor, 13, 103–5, 139, 142–43, 144
Romero, Oscar, 81n14

sacrificial citizenship, 57
Sagato, Rita, 101
Samaritans, 87
Santos, Boaventura de Sousa, 17, 133
School of Translators (Toledo), 32
Second Convivialist Manifesto, 36, 37
sensitive reasoning, 138
sensory investment accessing, 138
sentipensante (feeling-thinking), 134
sentipensar, 134
separation, 98
sharing the "mate," 8
Simpson, Leanne Betasamosake, 37
social engagement, 66–67
social interactions, 5, 28, 30
social justice, 53
social responsibility, 53, 54, 61, 65, 67–68
social transformation, 119
sociocultural theory, 60n19
soft eyes, 96
solidarity, 63, 122–26, 141
Spanish Inqusition, 32–33
spirituality, 42
standardized testing, 68
students, emotional needs of, 96
subjectivity, 53n5
Suess, Paulo, 41
sulear, 108–10
Suma Qamaña, 41
Sumak Kawsay, 41

surplus vision, 3
survivance, 8
suspending the sky, 128
sycamore trees, 95
symbállein, 38
symbol, 38

teachers, 13, 94–95, 140. *See also* educators
technological development, 33–34, 100–101
Teko Porã, 39–40, 46
tenderness, 138
Teresa of Calcutta, Madre, 81n14
tolerance, 44
Tools for Conviviality (Illich), 33–34
training, educating *versus,* 60n20
transformation, solidarity as framework for, 122–26
transformative praxis, 121
trees, comparison of, 95
Tronto, Joan, 72, 75–76
Truth, Sojourner, 81n14
Tubman, Harriet, 81n14
Turner, Victor, 98
Tutu, Desmond, 81n14

Umntu ngumtu ngabantu, 47
understanding, development of, 55
unity, 20–21
untested feasibility *(inédito viável),* 105, 142

Viveret, Patrick, 34
Vizenor, Gerald, 8
vulnerability, 74

wanderings, 106
Watson, Fiona, 19
Western academicism, 133
Western expansion, 65
wisdom, 16
world, love for, 116. *See also* earth

Yanomami people, 19

Zinn, Howard, 55

www.ingramcontent.com/pod-product-compliance
Lightning Source LLC
Chambersburg PA
CBHW071456150426
43191CB00008B/1364